LANDMARK VISITORS GUIDE

Côte d'Azur

Richard Sale

A research scientist before concentrating on travel
writing and photography, Richard's titles for Landmark
include the Cotswolds, Dorset, Italian Lakes,
Madeira, Provence and Somerset.

Mercantour National Park

Valberg
Beuil
St Sauveur
St Martin-Vesubie
N2205
Roquebillière

Tende
St Dalmas-de-Tende
Mount Bego
Vallée des Merveilles
Saorge

Gorges de Dalius
River Var
Gorges du Cians
Gorges de Vesubie

Breil-sur-Roya

Puget Théniers
N202

Sospel

ITALY

S20

Levens
N

W   E

S

L'Escaréne

D2204
Peillon
La Turbie

San Remo

N85

N202

A8

Menton
Roquebrune
MONTE-CARLO

Gourdon
Vence
Eze
MONACO
Beaulieu-sur-Mer

Tourettes-sur-Loup
St Paul
N7
NICE

St Vallier-de Thiey
D2085
Cagnes

Cap Ferrat

Grasse
Biot
Villeneuve-Loubet

N85
Vallauris

D562
Mougins

Golfe Juan
Antibes
Juan-le-Pins

A8/E80
CANNES
Cap d'Antibes

La Napoule
Ile de Lérins

Miramar
Le Trayas

Agay
N98

Fréjus
St Raphael
Côte de L'Esterel

St Aygulf

St Maxime
Pt. Grimaud

St Tropez

| 0 | | 8 | | 16miles |
| 0 | | 8 | 16km | |

Côte d'Azur

Opposite page: The Carlton Hotel, Cannes, one of the most famous on the Riviera
Right: Volleyball on the beach at St Raphaël

Côte d'Azur

Richard Sale

• Contents •

The Riviera was created by the rich and famous to give themselves somewhere to go to escape the harshness of their own winters. But it was not enough just to sit in a villa and wait for good weather back home. The rich needed to be entertained. It was the start of an industry which is still the raison d'être of the area. If you are looking for non-stop entertainment possibilities then this is the place for you.

To lose money while you are enjoying yourself, there are casinos in all the main towns: Antibes, Beaulieu, Cannes (several, most famously those at the Hôtel Carlton and the Palais des Festival), Grasse, Juan-les-Pins, Mandelieu-La Napoule, Menton, Monaco (the Monte-Carlo Casino is the most famous in Europe, if not the world, but there are several others, including one in the Café du Paris) and Nice (Casino Ruhl on Promenade des Anglais).

There are also plenty of nightclubs, all the major towns and larger hotels having at least one. In Cannes, The Hôtel Noga Hilton has an excellent Piano Bar (Le Grand Bleu). There is live music at the Actor's Bar, 84 Boulevard de la Croisette and dancing at the Palace Club in Avenue de Madrid.

In Nice there are regular cabarets at the Casino Ruhl and at Le Charlot in Rue St François de Paule. More subdued are the piano-bars of which there are a number of very good examples. Try Le Mississippi at 5 Promenade des Anglais or Le Baccara in the Hôtel Méridien at 1 Promenade des Anglais.

In Monaco Harry's in Avenue des Spelugues is an excellent piano-bar while Sass Café in Avenue Princess Grace has live music.

For the younger set all the main towns have discos. In Cannes try Jimmy's de Regne at the Palais des Festivals, Jane's Club at the Hôtel Gray d'Albion in Rue de Serbes or L'Opera in Rue Lecerf.

If you are in Nice, there are several good discos in Quai des États-Unis. Try L'Inferno at No. 2 or Toucan's Club at No. 73. In the old town Haute Tension at 2 Rue Tour is worth an ear as is Le Salon at 2 Rue Bréa. Live rock is played at Chez Wayne in Rue de la Préfecture.

There are also plenty of discos in Monaco. Current hot spots include Jimmy'z and Parady's, both at 26 Avenue Princesse Grace and The Living Room at 7 Avenue des Spelugues.

Not surprisingly there are also good times in St Tropez. Papagayo is the most popular at the moment, but Les Caves du Roy in the Hôtel Byblos is best if you want to rub shoulders with the rich and famous. Also there is the Café de Paris, a live rock café.

The Casino, Monte Carlo

*I*ntroduction

HISTORY

In the nineteenth century, anxious to avoid the severity of the British winter, the aristocracy 'discovered' the south of France, where the climate allowed health to be restored and a more gracious lifestyle to be observed. At first they headed for Nice, then part of Savoy, once a country in its own right but then part of the Kingdom of Sardinia. Later, when Savoy closed its borders to visitors to avoid contamination by a cholera outbreak in France, Lord Brougham found Cannes and increased the length of coast which the British could take-over for their winter sojourn in the sun. Railways increased the numbers who could come, the protracted coach journeys having dissuaded many. Queen Victoria came by royal train and the coast became the winter playground of the British social scene.

By 1887, by which time the area had been restored to France and the first casino had been opened in Monaco, there was an English newspaper, a cricket club in Cannes and hotels were springing up along the coast to cater for the rich new patrons. And in that year Stephen Liégard, a now largely forgotten poet and journalist, coined the name 'Côte d'Azur'. As with all such contrived names – particularly those attached to tourist spots – it has its detractors, but the name does seem to be appropriate. In the strong, overhead sun of the Mediterranean coast, the sea really is azure blue.

Arrival of the Russians

After the British came the Russians, an apparently limitless group of dukes, grand dukes and so on with ever more glorious titles, whose wealth created renewed prosperity and whose eccentricity even outdid the British. With them came the cream of the Russian art world. Stravinsky, Pavlova and Nijinsky all came to join Diaghilev in Monaco, making it (briefly) the world focus for ballet. But the coast, the Riviera as the British called it, requisitioning the Italian word for the seashore and imbuing it with upper-class meaning, was still a winter playground. In summer the heat and the mosquito-ridden swamps repelled all attempts to create a year-long colony.

The rich and famous arrive

All that changed in the 1920s when refrigeration allowed ice cubes to be made so that drinks could be chilled to just the right temperature for refined living and DDT eliminated the insects. The Americans arrived and brought the new technological order to the coast, creating a new summer playground and populating it with the famous as well as the rich. The war years stopped the flow of visitors and though it began again in the 1950s the scene had moved elsewhere. But then in 1956 Brigitte Bardot brought her bikini to St Tropez and the Riviera was fashionable again. The Film Festival at Cannes, the Grand Prix at Monaco, and other highlights of the social calendar have ensured that it has remained so.

Today the Riviera coast is a fabled land of conspicuous wealth, of celebrities, parties and fun. All of that is true, the visitor being virtually assured of a hot sun shining down from a blue sky and of almost limitless potential for entertainment. But in addition to this paradise of warm sea (a sea that, being nearly landlocked, has a tide which can be measured in fractions of an inch and so has no tidal drag to capture the unwary), sand and sun there is a history of art that is virtually unrivalled: every major artist of the first half of the twentieth century, the golden age of 'modern' art, came to the Côte d'Azur, each leaving his own contribution. The reason was the light, that special quality of clear light that artists loved but which is so difficult to describe.

Of course the popularity of the coast has its drawbacks. It is densely populated, almost a conurbation between Cannes and Menton with driving and parking presenting the familiar difficulties. There are times when the visitor can share Sam Goldwyn's legendary view of the value of a Riviera holiday – 'Nobody goes there anymore, it's too crowded.'

The Côte d'Azur coast

Pedantically the name Côte d'Azur applies only to the Riviera coast between Menton and Cannes (and so corresponds to the coastal section of the département of Alpes-Maritime). But such a definition ignores history and no one could take seriously a book on the area which does not include St Tropez. The coast from Menton to St Tropez is the subject of this book, the chapters being based on the main resorts – Nice, Cannes, Monaco – and following the coastline to its logical Riviera endpoints at Menton and St Tropez. For relief from the hedonism of the coast, trips inland are suggested. The picturesque hill villages of the Maritime Alps and the scenic beauties of the Mercantour National Park are not only a complete contrast to the sublime delights of the coast but help to make the Côte d'Azur one of the finest holiday areas in Europe.

Above: Cours Saleya in Nice's Old Town

Right: Promenade des Anglais, Nice

Below: The beach below Quai des Etats-Unis, Nice

1 Nice

Nice styles itself the Queen (occasionally Capital) of the Riviera, a title that would doubtless be disputed by Cannes but one that sits well on the elegant shoulders of France's premier tourist town: after Paris, Nice is the most visited town in the country.

NICE

N
W — E
S

0 ———— 0.5 miles
0 ———— 0.5 km

KEY

Attractions
① Gare Nice Ville
② Russian Cathedral
③ Masséna Museum
④ Place Masséna
⑤ Town Hall
⑥ Church of St Francois-de-Paul
⑦ Opera House
⑧ Gallery Dufy / Mossa
⑨ Cours Saleya
⑩ Naval Museum
⑪ Cathedral St Réparate
⑫ Lascaris Palace
⑬ Place Garibaldi
⑭ Beaux Arts Museum
⑮ Theatre de Verdure

Beaches
1 Florida Beach
2 Voilier Beach
3 Forum Beach0
4 Neptune Beach
5 Blue Beach
6 Sporting Beach
7 Libo Beach
8 Ruhi Beach
9 Galion Beach
10 Beau Rivage Beach
11 Opéra Beach
12 Castel Beach

HISTORY

The Terra Amata Museum on the east side of the port is built around the remains of a human settlement dating back 400,000 years, one of the oldest known traces of mankind in Europe. The remains include a fire and smoke stained hearth and a footprint preserved in limestone. The history of the town now takes a giant time step forward to about 1000BC when the Ligureans had a settlement on the side of the valley of the Paillon, a river which now reaches the Mediterranean out of sight of most visitors, the final stretch to its mouth hidden beneath the parkland of Espace Masséna and the Théâtre de Verdure.

Later, in about 400BC, Greeks from Marseille founded a trading post at the mouth of the river naming it from *Nikaîa* – victory, though quite which victory this might have been has never been established – or, and more likely, *Nîkaia*, a water sprite. When the Romans came they settled at Cimiez, at the northern end of today's city, perhaps as a precaution against sea-borne raiders. If that was the reason for the inland settlement it worked until the legions had retreated over the Alps to defend Rome against the barbarian hordes. Then the seaborne marauders sacked Cimiez.

So effective was the destruction that when the Counts of Provence resettled the Baie des Anges – as the sheltered bay between the headlands of Cap Ferrat and Cap d'Antibes is known – it was Nice they developed. By the mid-fourteenth century the town had grown into the third largest in Provence (after Marseille and Arles), but its population of 12,000 or so was then decimated by the Black Death.

Disillusioned by the catastrophe of the plague and by civil wars in Provence, the town decided to leave the province and negotiated with Count Amadeus VII of Savoy to become part of his domain. In 1388 he rode into the town: he is said to have been greeted not only by a thronging mass of cheering Niçois but by banners, garlands of flowers and a host of heavenly cherubs suspended on ropes and waving palm leaves. The Saviour, it seemed, had come.

The nineteenth century

Nice remained a Savoy town until 1860 except for a short period after the Revolution when, in 1792, it became part of the *département* of Alpes-Maritimes, Napoleon Bonaparte being stationed in the town. In 1814, Nice was returned to Savoy. Prince Maurice de Talleyrand, Napoleon's Foreign Minister who oversaw the return, is said to have been appalled when he first visited the area, claiming that had he been aware just how beautiful it was he would never have consented to its loss.

In 1859, France signed a treaty with the Sardinians under which, in exchange for French help to expel the Austrians from northern Italy, Savoy (by then under Sardinian control) would be ceded to France. The war that followed played a significant part in the *Risorgimento*, as the re-unification of Italy was called, and also saw, as a result of the suffering of the wounded after the battle of Solferino, the birth of the Red Cross.

But the Treaty of Villefranche which ended the fighting did not achieve all its aims. The Austrians still held Venice even though the French took Savoy. As a consequence, in 1860 there was a plebiscite of the townsfolk of Nice and the remnant of Savoy. By a vote of almost 26,000 to 260 the people voted to become (or stay in view of the events of 1859) French. At a ceremony on 12 September 1860 the Emperor Napoleon III and Empress Eugénie were handed the symbolic keys of the town, handcrafted in silver gilt.

The ceremony took place in what is now Place Garibaldi, the name a dreadful irony. Giuseppe Garibaldi had been born in Nice and having spent much of his adult life fighting for a united Italy he was mortified at his beloved home town being given away to the French. Before his death in 1882, Garibaldi spent several years fighting the French, attempting to force them out of the Papal States: if only it was possible to hear his thoughts on the naming of a square in his memory.

Nice today

Since the vote of 1860 the town has prospered and expanded. It is now the second city of the Mediterranean coast (after Marseille) and the fifth biggest city in France. In part its prosperity was due to the activities of Jean Médecin and his son Jacques, mayors for several decades from the late 1920s. Though embarrassingly right wing (Nice was twinned with

• THE NICE CARNIVAL •

A carnival in the town is mentioned as early as the thirteenth century, though today's celebrations date from 1873 when the artist Alexis Mossa revived it. A fortnight before Lent, King Carnival (*Sa Majesté Carnival*), a giant figure is set up in Place Masséna and presides over various events including the procession of the *Grosses Têtes*, people sporting giant papier-mâché heads. Then on Mardi Gras (Shrove Tuesday) King Carnival is taken to the beach and ceremoniously burned during a huge firework festival. On Ash Wednesday there is the frenetic Battle of Flowers.

Cape Town at the height of the Apartheid era and hosted events by the National Front) and, ultimately, proved to be corrupt, the near dictatorial rule of the Médecins brought new industries and wealth to the town, the cash being converted into new roads and developments which have enhanced its appeal. Today Nice is both a light industrial and commercial focal point, and a tourist town, the combination giving it a vibrancy occasionally lost in places that are wholly given over to tourism.

PROMENADE DES ANGLAIS

All visitors to Nice should walk along the Promenade des Anglais, one of the great streets of France (and Europe) though the double lanes of traffic in each direction detract from the quiet stroll the name would imply. Until a few years ago parking was allowed on the side of the wide seaside pavement but that, thankfully, has now been banned. The roadways themselves are separated by a central reservation of extravagant width which is planted with trees and shrubs so that the lanes look like the two halves of a Roman chariot circuit and the visitor could be forgiven fot thinking that that the cars circle endlessly. Ignore the noise and enjoy the view.

The road's name remembers the building of the town's first seaside promenade by the British in the late eighteenth century. Before that the poor tracks by the sea and the uneven nature of the shore allowed thieves and beggars to lie in wait for the rich visitors. They were persuaded to do something for the local economy by paying the poor to lay paving along the seafront. It was the first act of an aristocracy which was to bring prosperity to Nice.

The first English tourist to have left a record was Tobias Smollet travelling in 1763. Smollet found Nice typically Italian and was thrilled with the climate (he arrived in December but found the temperature delightfully warm) and the fact that oranges and lemons grew in the area. He liked the food and the fact that crime was almost unknown. It seems he was rather better pleased with Savoyan Nice than he had been with the France which he had visited on route to arrive there. In France, he noted sourly, the ground was usually ploughed by a team comprising a jackass, a he-goat and a lean cow harnessed together.

Origins of the Promenade

Following the publication of Smollet's book on his travels others began to journey south to escape the harshness of the British winter. The railway reached Nice in 1864 allowing travel times to be dramatically shortened and increasing the flow of British tourists.

With the arrival of Queen Victoria on the Riviera in 1882 the area's social standing was assured. The Queen's journey down through France was rather like the progress of medieval monarchs through their realms. On one occasion she granted an audience to the French President in her train while it was standing close to Paris for the night. The Queen offered him a seat. Doubtless the British thought the President should comprehend the graciousness of this offer which was not made to just anyone: it seems not to have occurred to them that as President of the country in which the Queen's train was stationed such an offer was the very least that should have been made.

On other occasions the Queen received the President at her hotel in Nice – paying him the compliment of greeting him at the door of her drawing room rather than making him wait. She usually stayed at the Excelsior Regina, the addition to the name reflecting her stays. The building is still there, close to the Matisse Museum in Cimiez, but it ceased to be a hotel long ago, becoming a hospital and then private apartments.

The British also treated the locals as they would the populace back home, a fact which caused a certain amount of resentment to a people who had chopped the head off a king in order to stop being treated that way again. But despite these inconveniences the relationship was a good one, the British were relieved of the tedium of winters back home, the locals became rich. The Promenade des Anglais is a tribute to that wealth creation.

WALKING DOWN THE PROMENADE DES ANGLAIS

The Promenade is a long road, stretching all the way from the airport to the Harbour (though it changes name for the last few hundred yards, becoming the Quai des États-Unis, a celebration of the Americans who created the summer Riviera as opposed to the winter holiday destination). Only the strong-willed would walk the entire length, but any walk will do. Heading into the town, to the right is the turquoise sea beyond a beach which is surprisingly narrow and pebbly: the Nice of the Victorians

was not a place for sunbathing or swimming.

They would not know today's beach where the sunseekers gather in force. There are public areas of beach but many private areas too. Here, for a fee, visitors can relax in the sun beds with their own private parasol, ordering drinks and food from private kitchens and enjoying private access to the sea. Fees are for the day or half day and all drinks etc are extra. The private areas are where the parasailing is found, the canopies adding vivid patches to the intensely blue sky. Suspended from a 'chute towed by a speedboat, the intrepid can enjoy aerial views of Nice for a few minutes. The take-off is sudden, the landing invariably wet, but the ride sensational.

Promenaders on the seaside pavement must beware of the roller bladers: there are cyclists too, but occasionally these are not what they seem: the young men in the smart shorts and shirts are likely to be police, Nice having learnt that the best way to patrol the Promenade is lightly clad and on two quick wheels. Strollers are treated to a summer fashion show by the young of Nice and Europe and the chance to watch the young and beautiful playing beach volleyball.

To the left, beyond the endless streams of traffic is a superb array of late nineteenth century and *belle époque* buildings, the latter including the fabled Negresco Hotel. (The traffic is not a new phenomenon, the movers and shakers of the early twentieth century drove their cars up and down too: in 1927 Isadora Duncan had her neck broken here one day when the trailing end of her fashionable scarf caught in the wheel of her Bugatti).

Hotel Negresco

Henri Negresco, a Romanian-born gypsy violinist, seeing the potential of a luxury hotel in Nice hired the Parisian architect Eduard Niermans, famous for having designed the Moulin Rouge, to build him a magnificent hotel. Niermans chose the fashionable *belle époque* style and created a masterpiece of the form. The hotel was completed in 1912: before Negresco had made enough to cover his debts war kept his customers at home. Sadly, he went bankrupt and died in poverty in Paris in 1920. But his hotel and his idea lived on, the Negresco becoming one of the great hotels of Europe.

Inside the guest rooms are museums to different periods of French style, while the public rooms contain original works by artists as famous as Picasso and Cocteau. The royal saloon has a 16,000-stone chandelier made for a Tsar and the lavatories on the ground floor are more lavishly ornamented than many other hotel lounges: they have been compared approvingly with salons in the Palace of Versailles.

Just beyond the Negresco is another fine nineteenth century mansion, Palais Masséna, in Italianate style. It was built by the great-grandson of Marshal Masséna, another famous military son of Nice. The marshal was said by Wellington to have been second only to Napoleon in military genius. The mansion now houses a small museum to Masséna (**Musée d'Art et d'Histoire,**

entrance in Rue de France at the back of the building) including a bust of him by Canova. There is also a collection of Napoleona, a fine collection of European Primitive artwork and some religious items including a silver and enamel reliquary and the early stone Virgin. The Palais also has a collection of work by local artists.

Further on is the Palais de la Méditerranée though only the façade of the 1920s building of Charles and Marcel Delmas remains, one of the best examples of Art Deco in the town. Once it housed a casino, now behind the façade a conference complex is being erected. The Promenade now reaches the Théâtre de Verdure where the Paillon river flows underground to reach the sea. Ahead now is Quai des États-Unis and the old town of Nice.

A TOUR OF THE OLD TOWN

At the eastern end of the sea front lies Vieux Nice, the old town. If the Promenade is the sunlovers' Nice and the pedestrianised area near Place Masséna the shoppers' Nice, then the old town is the Nice for explorers who will fall in love with its mix of Italianate and French style buildings, fine open squares and array of pavement cafés and good restaurants.

Promenade des Anglais leads into Quai des États-Unis. The sea is still to the right, while to the left are several interesting buildings.

The Opera dates from the 1880s, though Italian opera companies were performing in Nice from much earlier to entertain the rich winter visitors. On the corner where the dual carriageway (that will become Promenade des Anglais) starts is the arcaded Les Ponchettes (named for

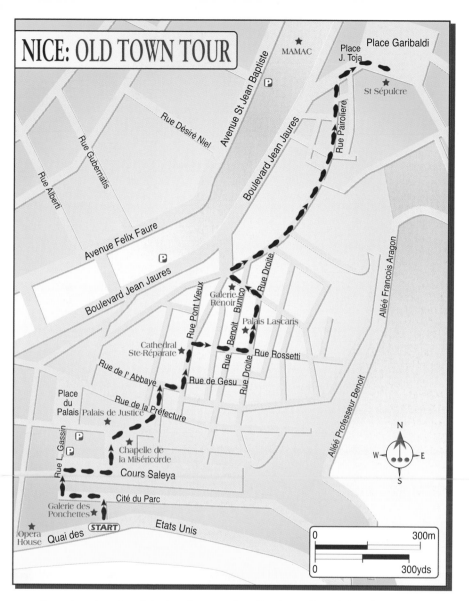

NICE: OLD TOWN TOUR

MAMAC

Place Garibaldi

Place J. Toja

St Sépulcre

Rue Pairoliere

Avenue St Jean Baptiste

Rue Désiré Niel

Boulevard Jean Jaures

Rue Gubernatis

Rue Alberti

Avenue Felix Faure

Rue Droite

Galerie Renoir

Rue Pont Vieux

Rue Benoit Bunico

Palais Lascaris

Cathedral Ste-Réparate

Rue de l'Abbaye

Rue de Gesu

Rue Droite

Rue Rossetti

Alléé Francois Aragon

Boulevard Jean Jaures

Place du Palais

Palais de Justice

Rue de la Préfecture

Allée Professeur Benoit

Rue L. Gassin

Chapelle de la Miséricorde

Cours Saleya

N
W E
S

Galerie des Ponchettes

Cité du Parc

START

Opera House

Quai des

Etats Unis

0   300m
0   300yds

the pointed rocks of the local coastline). This houses the **Gallery-Museum Raoul Dufy**, a collection of paintings, drawings, engravings and ceramics by an artist whose exuberant style captured the essence of Riviera café society in the early years of the twentieth century. Further along Les Ponchettes, at No. 59, there is another art gallery, the **Gallery-Museum Mossa**. This has collections of work by Alexis Mossa and his son Gustav-Adolf, the former an artist in the classical style, an expert of landscapes and carnival scenes, the latter in similar style at first, but developing a symbolic art with surrealist overtones.

Old Nice lies behind Les Ponchettes and should be explored at leisure. Close to Quai des États-Unis and running parallel to it is Cours

*Whether on the walkway (above) or the beach below it (below),
the Promenade des Anglais is the place to be seen*

Saleya in which is the Marché aux Fleurs, the Nice flower market, a wonderfully vibrant place. The flower sellers are adept at wrapping the displays for air travel so it is possible to buy souvenirs here. Beyond the flowers is the Marché des Antiquités, the antique market. There are other antique shops locally as well as some of the best of the old town's restaurants and cafés.

On the inland side of the flower market is the Chapelle de la Miséricorde of the Black Penitents, designed in 1740 by the Italian Guarini, in stunning Baroque style. Walk through Place Pierre Gautier beside the chapel and bear right to reach Place du Palais overlooked by the Palais du Justice built in the eighteenth century as the seat of local government.

Cathedral of Ste Réparte

From the far end of the *place*, turn right along Rue de la Préfecture, then left to reach the **Cathedral of Ste Réparte**, a glorious example of seventeenth century Baroque topped with a fine dome and lantern. Inside, the whole cathedral is in the most flamboyant of Baroque styles, but be sure to see the chapel of St Sacrament where the Baroque reaches new heights.

RUE ROSETTI TO PLACE GARIBALDI

From the delightful Place Rosetti on the eastern side of the cathedral, take Rue Rosetti to reach **Palais Lascaris**, in Rue Droite (but, to our left). The palace was built in Genoese Baroque style in the mid-seventeenth century. Behind the lovely façade is a wealth of period decoration and furniture. Especially good are the magnificent staircase and the *trompe l'oeil* ceiling. On the ground floor is a reconstructed eighteenth century pharmacy from Besançon.

Cuisine Nissard

Niçois cooking reflects the Italian heritage of the town, with house special ravioli and gnocchi, and a ratatouille to end them all with tomatoes, red peppers, courgettes/zucchini, onions and garlic cooked separately and then fried together. For starter how could you avoid trying a *salade Niçoise* (peppers, tomatoes, celery, black olives, onion, small artichokes (in season) and either boiled eggs or tuna. As an alternative starter try *soupe au pistou,* a thick vegetable soup to which the *pistou*, a sauce of garlic, basil and cheese, is added at serving.

For the main course try *porquetta*, stuffed suckling pig, or, if you are really brave, *tripes à la Niçoise*, tripe with a tomato sauce. For vegetable battered, deep fried courgette/zucchini flowers are something you may not find too often elsewhere.

Recently, to generate a new enthusiasm for traditional cooking, for the benefit of visitors and locals alike, an initiative to promote Cuisine Nissarde has begun. Look for the Cuisine Nissarde sticker in a restaurant to be assured that the ingredients and methods of preparation are authentic.

Continue along Rue Droite. At the next junction a left turn reaches the **Galerie Renoir** in Rue de la Loge, a municipal gallery with frequent exhibitions. Continue along Rue Droite, then bear right to reach Place St François, continuing ahead along Rue Pairolière. A short step right from here reaches the **Church of St Martin and St Augustine** the oldest of Nice's church. Martin Luther, then an Augustinian monk, celebrated mass in the church in 1510 and Garibaldi was baptised here in 1807.

Bear right at the end of Rue Pairolière to reach Place Garibaldi laid out in Piedmonte style at the end of the eighteenth century and overlooked by a statue of the great man. On the southern edge of this fine square is the **Church of St Sépulcre**, a chapel of the Blue Penitents built in Neo-classical style. Inside there is a very fine Assumption by Louis-Michel Van Loo. Close to the northwest corner is the **Musée Barla**, Nice's Natural History Museum. Apart from the usual exhibits, the museum has a collection of 7,000 plaster fungi. From the museum it is a short step to the MAMAC.

THE CASTLE AND THE PORT

Visitors who continue along Quai des États-Unis eventually reach the Château, the name given to the oval hill which rises 300ft (90m) above the sea. The name commemorates the castle that once topped it, though that was destroyed in 1706 on the orders of Louis XIV.

There is a lift to the top where there are the ruins of an eleventh century cathedral and a panorama dial to aid with picking out aspects of the exceptional view of the city.

There is an artificial waterfall and a cemetery which includes the grave of Mercedes Jellinek whose first name is said to have inspired that of the famous make of German car.

Close to the lift's bottom station there is the **Musée de la Marine**, the naval and marine museum, housed in the sixteenth century Bellanda Tower. The composer Hector Berlioz once lived here, but the collections are exclusively marine-based, with model ships, navigational equipment, naval weaponry and interesting displays on modern racing and pleasure craft.

The castle can be descended on its eastern side to reach the Harbour, a good alternative to the road around the seaward side. The road changes here, the Quai des États-Unis becoming the Quai Rauba Capeu, the hat thief. Follow the road around this wind-trapping headland and you'll see why.

Red-stucco, arcaded buildings line one side of the Harbour, Bassin Lympia (the port of limpid waters named from the marshy land which was drained and excavated in the 1750s to create the port), from which the boats for Corsica leave. A plaque on the house at the corner of Quai Papacino marks the house where Garibaldi was born.

On the far side of the port is the **Terra Amata Museum**, with its Palaeolithic finds, above which are Mont Alban and Mont Boron both of which offer wide views of the coast.

PLACE MASSÉNA AND CENTRAL NICE

From the Théâtre de Verdure the gardens of Jardin Albert I (the Three

Graces fountain here was sculpted by Volti) can be followed to Place Masséna from which the linear park of the Espace Masséna and Promenade du Paillon head north, sat on top of the Paillon river. This is a lovely area, open and airy, with fountains taking a little from the heat of the day: the bronze horses in the vast fountain in Place Masséna represent the planets of the solar system.

When viewing the 24 ton 'Arc' of Bernard Venet, which is 62ft (19m) high and 125ft (38m) long, and the buildings of the MAMAC, it is difficult to remember that the Place Masséna was actually laid out in 1835 and completed by the 1850s. The MAMAC is the local name for the **Musée d'Art Moderne et d'Art Contemporan,** the four leaden marble towers linked by transparent passageways, the work of Yves Bayard and Henri Vidal. Entry is by way of a huge piazza, the collections including works by *avant garde* artists and those of the Pop Art movement. There is also an important collection of works by Yves Klein. The building itself has its lovers and detractors – rather like the works it houses.

Galleries Lafayette, the famous French departmental store, stands at the northern corner of the Place Masséna, filling one block of Avenue Jean Médecin which runs northward from the square. The Avenue is the main shopping street of Nice, together with the pedestrianised streets which head west from the square, Rue Masséna and Rue de France (which run parallel to Promenade des Anglais) and side streets running from them. Here too are the best of the pavement cafés, the lack of traffic (and its inevitable noise) adding to the joys of people-watching.

At the top of Avenue Jean Médecin, to the right, a short walk reaches the **Musée National Message Biblique Marc Chagall.**

Marc Chagall and the Biblical Message

Marc Chagall was born to a poor Jewish family in Russia in 1887, moving to Paris and then to southern France when he followed his vocation as a painter. He died in St Paul in 1985.

His art is usually classified as Primitive, but such groupings are not always helpful. It is better, perhaps, to see Chagall as having maintained a child-like wonder for scenes and events, portraying them in an equally child-like way, both in form and in tone, the latter usually being very vivid. During the years from 1954 to 1967, Chagall painted the 17 huge canvases which form the basis of the museum, these depicting scenes from the Books of Genesis and Exodus, and the Song of Songs. It is interesting to note that Chagall has included many Christian symbols in these essentially Jewish stories. The whole – canvases, setting and the somewhat severe building – represent a remarkable artistic statement of faith.

Russian Orthodox Cathedral

A turn left at the top of the Avenue leads to Nice station and, beyond it, the **Russian Orthodox Cathedral,** as surprising a building as can be found anywhere on the Riviera. This magnificent red brick and gray marble building – brilliantly set off by the six domes, each covered with ceramic tiles – was built in the early years of this century, at a time when the Russian aristocracy was supplanting the British as the mainstay of the local economy. The money was provided by Empress Maria Feodorovna, widow of Tsar Alexander III, and Tsar Nicholas II. The cathedral was built on land where the Villa Bermond had previously stood. It was in the villa that the eldest son of Tsar Alexander II had died in 1865 and the cathedral was in his memory. The cathedral was completed just five years before the Russian Revolution which saw the murder of the Tsar.

WESTERN NICE

Towards the western end of Promenade des Anglais, just north of the seafront in an area known as Les Baumettes, is the **Musée des Beaux Arts** (sometimes known as the Musée Chéret) with some good early works, particularly by seventeenth century Italian painters, a few by J H Fragonard, and a good collection of canvases by the Impressionists with whom the south of France is so readily associated – Degas, Dufy, Bonnard, Sisley and others.

Further west, towards the Nice-Côte d'Azur airport, is the **Musée International d'Art Naif Anatole Jakovsky**, a gallery of naive art established around the collection of Anatole Jakovsky. The collection comprises some works of Jakovsky himself, and some 600 by lesser known artists from all over the world. North of the Jakovsky collection is the **Miniature Train Museum** where models – not only trains but cars and airplanes – explore the history of transport.

Further west, still on the Promenade des Anglais, but directly opposite the airport, is the **Phoenix Parc Floral**, a phenomenal garden park. The external areas of garden, with lake, rockeries and numerous delightful features, are excellent, but the truly remarkable feature is the Astronomical Garden, the largest plant house in the world. This conical greenhouse is divided into seven sections each of which has its climate automatically controlled so as to simulate one of the world's tropical areas. As a consequence the visitor can wander through areas of tree ferns or among exotic orchids. The house also has collections of appropriate birds and insects: the butterflies alone making a visit worthwhile. Close to the Parc is Nice's newest museum, the **Musée des Arts Asiatiques** where collections of Chinese, Japanese, Cambodian etc

Parasailing is just one of the sports which can be enjoyed on Nice's beach

Henri Matisse

Henri Matisse was born in 1869 and became the leading member of *Les Fauves*, the savages, who transformed art in the early years of this century. Matisse's real talent was in decorative art and the blend of this form with the 'new' art which disregarded natural forms. Picasso, the other great artist of the twentieth century, extended the work of Cézanne, developing it into Cubism and beyond. Matisse pursued a different route, his art developing into even more decorative forms, as exemplified by the famous blue paper cut-out pictures. The visitor is greeted by one of Matisse's largest works, a paper cut-out maquette decorating the museum's entrance area. Beyond it are around 70 paintings and cut-outs, several hundred drawings and engravings and some artwork from Matisse's personal collection.

art from the sixth century onwards are housed in a superb new building.

NORTHERN NICE

The northern district of Nice is still called Cimiez, the name of the earliest Roman settlement. It is best approached from the Chagall Museum, following Boulevard de Cimiez north to the huge Hôpital de Cimiez, once the Excelsior Regina Hotel. Though still called the 'hospital' the building is now private apartments. Henri Matisse once lived in one of the apartments painting a mural on one wall which was removed when he left!

Bearing right at the old Regina brings the visitor to the **Musée Matisse**, housed in a vividly red seventeenth Genoese villa – though all is not quite as it seems, some of the apparent decoration being *trompe l'oeil*.

Beside the Matisse Museum's villa are the **Musée et Site Archéologiques**, the excavated remains of Roman *Cemenelum* (Cimiez) and a small museum which houses the better finds from the site. Also nearby is the Franciscan Monastery of Notre-Dame de l'Assumption (**Monastere de Cimiez**).

The monastery was founded in the ninth century by Benedictine monks, and taken over and restored by the Franciscans some 400 years ago. Within the abbey church are three superb works by Louis Bréa all dated to around 1475 – a Crucifixion, Deposition and Pietà. The monastery's museum (**Musée Franciscan**) explores the history of the Franciscans in Nice. Beside the monastery is a very quiet garden from which a cemetery is reached. Here lie Raoul Dufy, close to the entrance, and Henri Matisse, whose tomb is more difficult to locate, being at the lower level.

To the west of Cimiez, in the St Barthélemy district, close to Boulevard de Cessole, a continuation of Boulevard Gambetta which heads north from the station, is the Prieure du Vieux Logis, a priory created from a sixteenth century oil mill and housing some excellent medieval furniture and artwork. Close by **Villa Arson** is a lovely eighteenth century villa set in huge terraced gardens in part given over to a contemporary structure in concrete and pebbles. The villa is renowned for its promotion of contemporary art and houses frequent exhibitions.

The main shopping area of the town is concentrated on the pedestrianised area of Rue Masséna and Rue de France which runs parallel to Promenade des Anglais from Place Masséna. Rue Paradis, a turn seawards from Rue Masséna, is the place for fashion, **Chanel**, **Emporio Armani**, **Gladys Falk**, **Sonia Rykel**, all have stores there. **Yves St-Laurent Rive Gauche** is in Avenue de Suéde which also heads seawards from Rue Masséna, a little further along, while **Chacok**, a Niçoise fashion house, is in Espace Grimaldi at the end of Rue de France. Another Niçoise fashion house, **Claud Bonucci** can be found in Rue Massenet, off Rue de France. Slightly cheaper, but still at the classy end of the market, **Max Mara** has a store in Rue de la Liberté which runs parallel to Rue Masséna one street inland.

Leather goods

For leather goods, handbags etc, **Louis Vuitton** is also in Avenue de Suéde, while **Longchamp** is in Avenue de Verdun the road beside Jardin Albert 1er. Avenue de Verdun also has a number of less well-known, but very classy fashion stores.

Jewelry

Avenue de Verdun is still a top choice, **Cartier** having their store in the street, while **Rolex** are in Avenue de Suéde.

French goods

For typically French goods that are cheaper, **Galeries Lafayette** is the place, with a huge store on the inland side of Place Masséna. Other French departmental stores are **Nice Etoile** and **La Riviera**, both in Avenue Jean Médecin which heads inland from Place Masséna. In the same street there is a **Marks & Spencer**.

Antiques

For antiques it is best to explore the old town, though **Galerie des Antiquaires** at 7 Promenade des Anglais is very good.

Souvenirs

Souvenirs hunters have a virtually unlimited choice, but for interesting ideas try **Galeries Niçoises** in Place

Garibaldi on the edge of the old town. For wine and local spirits it is worth visiting **La Cave Bianchi** in Rue de la Terrasse in the old town (head north from the Opera). Olive oil, that other wonder of Provence can be found in the **Maison de l'Olive** in Rue Pairoliére in the old town. Those not able to make it to the perfumeries in Grasse itself should visit **Au Parfum de Grasse** in Rue St Gaétan in the northern part of the town. For the sweet tooth **Confiseries Florian** on Quai Papacino beside Bassin Lympia offers the visitor the chance to watch the making of crystallized flowers, fruit sweets and chocolates as well as the chance to buy them.

Galleries

The art lover is spoilt for choice, with dozens of galleries. The best are listed in **Les Galeries d'Art**, a brochure available at the Tourist Information Centre, but if you only have the chance to visit one, try **Galerie Art'7** at Promenade des Anglais, where a number of small galleries show contemporary art.

Markets

There are several markets in Nice which will be of interest even if you are not intending to buy. The **flower market** in Cours Saleya in the old town is wonderful: it is open all day every day except on Sunday and Monday afternoons. There are two flea markets: **Marché à la Brocante** on Mondays in Cours Saleya (all day Monday) and **Les Puces de Nice** in Place Robilante, also in the old town (Tuesday to Saturday, all day). There is also a daily (except Monday) street market for fruit and vegetables in Cours Saleya.

Galerie-Musée Mossa
59 Quai des États-Unis
Open: All year, Tuesday to Saturday
10am-12noon, 2-6pm; Sunday
2-6pm. ☎ 93 62 37 11

Galerie des Ponchettes/
Galerie Raoul Dufy
77 Quai des États-Unis
Open: All year, Tuesday to Saturday
10am-12noon, 2-6pm; Sunday
2-6pm. ☎ 93 62 31 24

Galerie Renoir
8 Rue de la Loge
Open: All year, Tuesday to Saturday
10.30am-1pm, 2-6pm.
☎ 93 13 40 46

Musée d'Archéologie
160 Avenue des Arènes de Cimiez
Open: All year (except 3 weeks in
November/December), April to
September Tuesday to Sunday
10am-1am, 2-5pm; October to
March Tuesday to Sunday 10am-
12noon, 2-5pm.
The archaeological site is open at
the same times. ☎ 93 81 59 57

Musée des Arts Asiatiques
405 Promenade des Anglais
Open: All year, May to mid-October
daily except Tuesday 10am-6pm;
mid-October to May daily except
Tuesday 10am-5pm.
☎ 92 29 37 00

Musée d'Art Moderne et d'Art
Contemporan (MAMAC)
Promenade des Arts
Open: All year, daily except Tuesday
11am-6pm (open until 10pm on
Fridays). ☎ 93 62 61 62

Musée d'Art Naïf
Anatole Jakovsky
Château Ste Hélène
Avenue Val Marie
Open: All year, daily except Tuesday
10am-12noon, 2-6pm.
☎ 93 71 78 33

Musée Barla
(Musée d'Histoire Naturelle)
60 Boulevard Risso
Open: All year, daily except Tuesday

**The Russian Orthodox
Cathedral**

10am-12noon, 2-6pm.
☎ 93 55 15 24

Musée des Beaux Arts
33 avenue des Baumettes
Open: All year, daily except Monday
10am -12noon, 2-6pm.
☎ 92 15 2 28

Musée Franciscain et
Monastére de Cimiez
Place du Monastère
Open: All year, daily except Sunday
10am-12.30pm, 3-7pm.
☎ 93 81 00 04

Musée Masséna
Palais Masséna
65 Rue de France
Open: All year (except for 2 weeks in
November), daily except Monday
10am-12noon, 2-6pm.
☎ 93 88 11 34

Musée Matisse
164 Avenue des Arènes de Cimiez
Open: All year, April to September
daily except Tuesday 10am-6pm;
October to March daily except
Tuesday 10am-5pm.
☎ 93 53 40 53

Musée des Trains Miniatures

Boulevard Impératrice Eugénie
Open: All year, April to September
Daily 9.30am-6.30pm; October to
March daily 9.30am-5pm.
☎ 93 97 41 40

Musée National Message Biblique Marc Chagall

Avenue du Docteur Ménard
Open: All year, July to September
daily except Tuesday 10am-6pm;
October to June daily except
Tuesday 10am-5pm. ☎ 93 53 87 20

Musée Naval

Tour Bellanda
Parc du Château
Open: All year, June to September
Wednesday to Sunday 10am-
12noon, 2-7pm; October to May
Wednesday to Sunday 10am-
12noon, 2-5pm. ☎ 93 80 47 61

Musée de Paleontotologie Humaine de Terra Amata

25 Boulevard Carnot
Open: All year, daily except Monday
9am-12noon, 2-6pm. ☎ 93 55 59 93

Palais Lascaris

15 Rue Droite
Open: All year (except November),
daily except Monday 10am-12noon,
2-6pm. ☎ 93 62 05 54

Phoenix Parc Floral

405 Promenade des Anglais
Open: All year, April to September
Daily 9am-7pm; October to March
daily 9am-5pm. ☎ 93 18 01 01

Prieuré du Vieux Logis

59 Avenue St Barthélemy
Open: All year, Wednesday, Thursday, Saturday and first Sunday of
the month 3-5pm.
☎ 93 88 44 74

Villa Arson

20 Avenue Stéphen Liégard
Open: All year, July to September
daily except Monday 1-7pm; October
to June Daily except Monday 1-6pm.
☎ 93 07 73 73

Restaurants

For genuine Cuisine Nissarde try:

La Petite Maison (FF)
3 Rue de l'Opera, ☎ 93 92 59 59

La Zucca Magica (F)
4bis Quai Papacino, ☎ 93 56 25 27

For more international cuisine try:

Chantecler (FFF)
Hotel Négresco
37 Promenade des Anglais
☎ 93 16 64 00
The most expensive place in town,
but which Michelin claims is worth
the detour. If at the end of the meal
you think a '0' has been added to
your bill by mistake, it hasn't been.

Don Camillo (FF)
5 Rue Ponchettes
☎ 93 85 67 95
Very good Italian cooking, but with
distinct Niçois overtones.

Les Pêcheurs (FF)
18 Quai des Docks
☎ 93 89 59 61
Excellent fish restaurant beside the
Bassin Lympia.

Merenda (F)
4 Rue de la Terrasse
(No phone)
Neat little Niçois restaurant in the old
town, behind the Opera.

From Nice, several journeys northwards enter the fine country of Haute-Provence. Perched villages, characteristic of Provence, are even more spectacular above the Côte d'Azur. At a distance they look ashen, aloof, even distrustful: they were built for protection against incessant invasion. Their thick walls, narrow, steep, twisting cobbled and arcaded streets, their tiny squares and fountains, clustering towards an ancient church, are a delight to explore. Many houses are now workshops for artist and artisans where paintings, ceramics, woven cloths, jewelry or olivewood carvings can be bought.

The perched village of Peillon

There is too much country to the north of Nice to cover each village, so a small number of excellent itineraries are suggested here.

TOUR 1 – VAR, VAÏRE, VERDON & ASSE VALLEYS BY TRAIN

One of the best uses the train rather than the car, the justly famous scenic journey by the Chemins de Fer de la Provence from Gare de Provence, Place de la Libération in Nice.

The train explores the valleys of the Var, Vaïre, Verdon and Asse rivers, going through Puget-Théniers, Entrevaux, Annot, Thorame-Haute, St André-les-Alpes and Digne. This journey is about 90 miles (150km) and takes just over 3 hours in each direction, so the return can be made on the same day.

The trip can be broken at any intermediate station: **Puget-Théniers** with its attractive old quarter;

One of the best perched villages lies very close to Nice. To reach **Peillon**, take the D2204 northwards towards L'Escarène, turning right, then right again towards the village. The road to the village offers superb views towards it (and rather pleasant smells from the Geriko coffee plant), but parking is very limited at its end – there is no car park and minimal roadside parking. The residents hope that an increase in tourism will be catered for by a shuttle bus up the hill. The village itself is so picturesque that words can barely do it justice – wander at will and be enchanted.

Close to Peillon is **Peille**, another wonderfully picturesque medieval village with a maze of tight streets and a charming twelfth century church with a Romanesque belltower. Inside there is a painting of medieval Peille which allows the visitor a direct comparison of the changes which have occurred over the centuries.

Entrevaux, once a frontier town between France and Savoy which Vauban turned into the almost perfect fortified town. The main gateway into Entrevaux offers one of the most dramatic entries into any town in France. Inside, the castle has a moat, a portcullis and plenty of cannons, and the views from it are stunning. The cathedral is also worth a visit for its exuberant Baroque interior.

Annot is a beautiful village which seems to grow out of the surrounding rocks: huge boulders, known as the *grés d'Annot* litter the streets. And finally **Digne**, at the heart of a lavender growing area.

TOUR 2 – LEVENS AND THE VÉSUBIE VALLEY

Take the N202 northwards, through pretty country, to Le Plan-du-Var, turning right there to drive through the narrow and winding, but beautiful **Gorges de la Vesubie** to reach St-Jean-la-Rivière. A right turn here leads to Duranus and the **Saut de Français**, a vertical drop where a group of soldiers were thrown to their deaths after being captured by local bandits.

Ahead now is **Levens**, a picturesque village with an array of terraced gardens. Little now remains of the medieval castle of the Grimaldis. Legend has it that the village folk, tired of one particularly tyrannical member of the family who had become their overlord threw him out one day and destroyed the castle. One stone, called the *boutau*, was kept as a memorial and a procession to it is made every year on St Antonin's day to celebrate the town's freedom from domination.

A left turn at St-Jean-la-Rivière leads up a narrow road not recommended to the faint-hearted to reach the sanctuary of **Madonna d'Utelle**, built in 1806 on the site of an earlier church (said to have been founded in the ninth century by a group of sailors in thanksgiving for having survived an appalling storm). The view of the Maritime Alps from the church is one of the best on the Côte d'Azur.

Northwards the beautiful Vésubie valley can be followed to Roquebillière. Just beyond the village the road forks: go right to follow the Vallon de la Gordolasque, a very picturesque valley, into the Mercantour National Park, passing the Cascade du Ray, a delightful pair of waterfalls. A left turn at the fork leads to **St Martin-Vésubie**, a starting point for climbers and walkers visiting the Maritime Alps. The pedestrian-only Rue du Docteur Cagnoli, leading to the church, is well worth exploring: set among its Gothic houses is the Chapel of the White Penitents with a bulb-shaped bell-tower.

St Martin is a cool alternative to the coast, but is almost at the limit of day trip exploration. Those with more time can go west to **St Saveur-sur-Tinée**, another picturesque village. North now are the ski resort of Isola 2000 (named for its height: 2,000m – 6,560ft) and Auron from where a funivia takes the visitor to the 8,115ft (2,474m) peak of Las Donnas, a memorable viewpoint. From St Saveur, a fine return to the coast is to go westwards to Beuil and south from there, through the beautiful Gorges du Cians.

TOUR 3 – NICE TO L'ESCARENÈ

Our final tour from Nice follows the D2204 past the turn to Peillon to reach **L'Escarène**, a pleasant town with a fine old single-arched bridge. Northwards now, along the D2566, is **Lucéram**, notable for the altarpieces and treasury in the church. The altarpieces are by Louis Bréa and pupils of his school. From Lucéram the poor, itinerant artists, commissioned by Penitent Brotherhoods and overshadowed by Italian Renaissance artists, carried their paints and brushes over mountain tracks from church to church. The treasury includes a beautiful fifteenth century silver statuette and several excellent reliquaries. North again lies **Pierre Plate** another fine viewpoint. To make a circular tour, return towards L'Escarène and turn left to Sospel, following the Vallée du Carai south to reach the A8 close to Menton.

V isitors seeking art and architecture, sun and sea, sports by the hundred – from a gently relaxing game of golf to the more hazardous pursuits of rock climbing and diving – are well served by the Riviera. Younger visitors may enjoy all of these too, but may also be interested in the following places which are more specifically aimed at them. Opening times are for the summer months.

Marineland Complex

On the N7 between Antibes and Villeneuve-Loubet-Plage
All the facilities are open from 10am daily.
☎ 93 33 49 49 is the general number for the complex.

The facilities include:

Marineland, with sharks, orca, dolphins, penguins and seals.
La Petite Ferme, a farm with goats, rabbits, horses, cows, chickens etc. There are pony tours on the farm, a nursery, mini-golf and a face-painting studio. ☎ 93 33 82 72.

La Jungle des Papillons, a tropical house with over 150 species of exotic butterflies, together with spiders (some huge and hairy) and turtles. ☎ 93 33 82 72.

Adventure Golf, the ultimate in crazy golf. Three courses of varying length and absurdity.

Aqua-Splash, an array of pools and water slides.

Aquatica

Near Fréjus
Another aqua park with slides and pools.
Open: daily 10am-6pm.
☎ 94 51 82 51

Luna Park

Close to the junction of the N98 and D559
Near Port Grimaud
Has typical fairground attractions. It opens evenings only, but that does have the advantage of big-wheel rides at night.
Open: daily from 8.30pm.
☎ 94 56 35 64

Kindia Park

Villeneuve-Loubet
With trampolines, paint balls, go-karts, a bouncy castle and some more adventurous rope swings for older children.
Open: daily from 9am.
☎ 93 65 61 92

Parc de Loisirs de Barbossi

On the N7 near Mandelieu-La Napoule
For younger children, with rides, electric cars, a little train and a pony club.
Open: daily from 1.30pm.
☎ 93 49 64 74

Koaland

Parc de la Madone
5 Avenue de la Madone
Menton
Mainly for younger children, with mini go-karts, rides and a goat pen.
Open: daily from 10am-12noon, 3-7pm. ☎ 92 10 00 40

Astorama

Éze
Has a planetarium and opportunities for observing stars and planets through big telescopes.
Open: daily from 6.30pm.
☎ 93 85 85 58

Visiobulle

Operates from the Courbet quay
Juan-les-Pins
This large glass-bottomed boat explores the coast of Cap d'Antibes offering a glimpse of the underwater world normally seen only by divers. The hull shape means that you can, if you wish, sit under the water. Trips daily from 9am to 6pm.
☎ 93 67 02 11

Aquascope

A glass-bottomed boat sails regularly from 9am-6pm from Quai Lunel in Nice.
☎ 92 00 42 30

Acti-Loisirs

Villefranche-sur-Mer
Daily whale and dolphin watching trips.
☎ 92 47 75 00

Go-karting

There are go-kart circuits near Cannes (Pilotez, 215 Avenue Francis Tonner, Cannes-La-Bocca, ☎ 93 47 88 88) and Bar-sur-Loup (Fun Kart, Plateau de la Sarrée, Route du Gourdon, ☎ 93 42 48 08) as well as smaller circuits in several other places. Juan-les-Pins has a track for smaller children on the seafront.

Model Railway Exhibition

Nice
Open: daily from 9.30am.
☎ 93 97 41 40

Model Railway Exhibition

N85 2.5 miles (4km) south of Grasse
Open: daily from 9.30am.
☎ 93 77 97 97

Zoos

Fréjus, Cap Ferrat and Monaco.

2

Heading west along the Promenade des Anglais the visitor reaches the airport and an entry to the A8 autoroute. This is the quickest way to Cannes, but misses much that is worth seeing.

CAGNES-SUR-MER

On the N98 coast road the first major town is Cagnes-sur-Mer, though the heart of the town is inland. Cagnes is a sprawling mass which has engulfed the chic racecourse, l'Hippodrome de la Côte d'Azur.

At Haut-de-Cagnes, which is the prettiest part of the town, is the castle of the Grimaldis who became lords of the town soon after taking Monaco in the early fourteenth century.

The castle is now the Château-Musée, worth visiting for its decorations, but also housing two museums. Of the decorations, the

finest is the Fall of Phaeton, an extraordinary *trompe l'oeil* ceiling by the Genoese artist Carlone. He is said to have wept when the work was completed as he would never see it again: within a few weeks he was dead.

One of the two museums is devoted to the olive tree, that veritable symbol of Provence. The other museum is of modern Mediterranean art, including works by some of the many painters who have been profoundly influenced by the light of this coast which is often called the 'Mecca of Modern Art'. During the summer the castle houses an exhibition of contemporary art.

The Renoir Museum

In Cagnes-Ville is the Renoir Museum, Avenue des Collettes, the house and garden where Renoir (1841-1919) spent the last 12 years of his life after being advised by his doctor to move to a warmer climate to alleviate the symptoms of his rheumatoid arthritis.

In the house everything has been left much as it was. There are the tools of his trade in the studio, a painting, some drawings and sculpture, correspondence, photographs and momentos. Saddest of the items are the Great Man's wheelchair and the photograph of his hands late in life.

During his last years his main solace was his paintings, but he could only work with his brushes tied to his hands. In the garden stands the *Venus Victrix*, the large bronze Venus that is Renoir's most famous sculpture. It overlooks a beautiful garden, well laid out with olive, lemon and orange trees.

The museum is a moving tribute to an artist who expressed his love for the freshness of life.

Renoir's studio has been left just as it was the last time he used it

ST PAUL

Inland from Cagnes are the twin towns of St Paul and Vence. St Paul has always been a little too far from the sea to share in much of the general prosperity, but it was discovered by artists in the 1920s and has been an artistic, rather than jet-set, destination ever since, that rebirth accounting for the huge number of art galleries in the village. For further proof, the visitor need look no further than the **Maeght Foundation**, a modern art museum set in a suitably designed building constructed in 1964. Some of the art on view is pleasantly displayed outdoors.

Artists represented in the museum include Bonnard, Braque, Chagall, Kandinsky and Miró, and the work includes not only paintings, but sculptures and stained glass as well. In the village there are fine views from the old ramparts, and the church is worth visiting for a fine painting of St Catherine of Alexandria attributed to Tintoretto. The museum of local history in the Place de la Castre explores facets of St Paul's history in eight dioramas.

VENCE

Though originally a Ligurean town, Vence was important in Roman times, and equally important in the early years of Christian France. In the Wars of Religion, the town was besieged by Huguenots but did not fall, a fact commemorated each Easter with a festival.

The visitor should definitely not miss the Old Town, which still has part of the original defensive wall and the old castle. The castle – built by the Barons of Villeneuve whose conflicts with the Bishops of Vence enrich the town's medieval history – houses the Fondation Emile Hugues, named for a former town mayor. There is a permanent art collection, but the Foundation chiefly exists to promote contemporary art by way of an annual series of exhibitions. The castle stands in Place du Frêne, named for the huge ash-tree that dominates it. The tree is said to have been planted to commemorate the visit of François I and Pope Paul III to the town.

Close by is the old cathedral, on the site of a Roman temple to Mars and an early, Merovingian, church. The cathedral is in fine Romanesque style.

Elsewhere, the Old Town is a delight, helped by the exclusion of cars – neatly tucked away in a car park beneath the Place du Grand Jardin. Place de Peyra, near the Porte de Peyra, has a fine fountain and many other little squares and alleys are equally delightful. It is no surprise to discover that Vence has attracted many artists and writers over the years. Dufy, André Gide and DH Lawrence all spent time here, the latter dying in Vence, of TB, in 1930.

VILLENEUVE-LOUBET

Heading back towards the coast, close to Cagnes is Villeneuve-Loubet, with an excellent culinary art museum in the house in which Auguste Escoffier (1846-1935), head of the most famous family in the history of cooking-as-art. There are all the things you would imagine in the world's most famous kitchen, together

The old town in Vence

Henri Matisse came to Vence in 1941, but was soon taken very ill. He was nursed back to health by the local Dominican sisters and in gratitude, between 1947 and 1951 he designed and decorated the Chapelle du Rosaire, north-west of the Old Town. "Despite its imperfections, I think it is my masterpiece" he said of the chapel, adding that it was the culmination of "a lifetime devoted to the search for truth".

The chapel is a simple, square, white building, the only clues to Matisse's work being the figures above the door, the white and blue tiled roof and the delicate wrought-iron cross that surmounts it. Inside, the simplicity is maintained, the murals being in black lines on white walls, the only tones coming from the sun through the stained glass windows. Of the murals, that depicting the Stations of the Cross is the most moving. Matisse is now considered to be one of the finest artists of the twentieth century, so the chapel should be high on the list of all visitors.

A work by Matisse on the outside of the Chapel of the Rosary

with exhibitions of sugar and almond paste work. For the gourmet and gastronomic connoisseur there are also 5,000 menus, some dating to the early nineteenth century. The town also has a military museum devoted to French involvement in twentieth century wars.

ON TO BIOT

On the coast road the view is now dominated by the Marina Baie des Anges at Villeneuve-Loubet-Plage. The four triangular blocks, each a gentle S bend, were designed by André Minangoy and are one of the most distinctive structures on the Riviera. The blocks have lovers and loathers: such is their dominance it is difficult to be neutral about them. Personally I would trade a winning lottery ticket for a penthouse at the top of one of the blocks (well, maybe).

The road now hugs the coast. The beach is public here, but is much more exposed than at Nice, that and the fact that it is vast, meaning it seems more sparsely peopled. If you like a lot of space this might be the place to try.

Soon, to the right are Marineland and the village of Biot.

Marineland

Europe's first marine zoo has dolphins, orca (killer whale), penguins, seals and sea lions. A newer attraction is *Sharks* where a transparent tunnel allows visitors to walk through the shark aquarium offering a real close up of the fish from all sides.

The site includes a small marine museum, one item of which is a model of Columbus' *Santa Maria* constructed from one and a half million matchsticks. Close to the site are several amusement parks, including Parc Aqua-Splash a water-based park with an array of slides and pools.

BIOT

Biot is surrounded by acres of carnations and roses destined for the Riviera flower markets. The ubiquitous and handsome terracotta vases that adorn many gardens once formed the main industry of Biot. The local history museum, beside the Tourist Information Office in the charming old village, explores the history of the town and the ceramics industry. A link, of sorts, with the old industry is still maintained as visitors can watch glass-making in the village, the factory being famous for Biot bubble glass.

ANTIBES

Continuing along the coast the view is now to old Antibes and its fortresses. Antibes has a very ancient history, having been the Greek port of Antipolis, founded in about the fourth century BC. In his early years as a general, Napoleon defended the Mediterranean coast from the town, though he was briefly imprisoned in Fort Carré after the fall of Robespierre. He received a hostile reception when he landed in Golfe Juan on his return from Elba. Fort Carré, to the north of the town, was built by Vauban: it is the most prominent part of what remains of the seventeenth century fortifications of the town.

Old town

Close to the port, which bears Vauban's name, is the old town, a delightful array of tight streets and alleys for the walker, an absolute nightmare for the driver with very few parking places and, often, illegally parked cars blocking the way. There is a great walk along the old ramparts with fine views of the port and of the town from above Porte Marine, the ancient gateway.

Within the old town there are several interesting museums. The **Musée Archéologique in Bastion St André** (another part of Vauban's work) explores the town's long history; the **Musée de la Tour** in the Orme Tower has a collection on local culture, with costumes and furniture. There are also Léo Roman's original water skis, the ones he used to invent the sport, at Juan-les-Pins, in 1921. The **Musée Peynet** is devoted to the curious, sentimental drawings of Raymond Peynet, the French creator of the famous lovers. The more famous Picasso museum is housed in the Château Grimaldi.

CAP D'ANTIBES

From Antibes it is possible to cut off the headland of Cap d'Antibes, going straight to Juan-les-Pins. But the road around the headland is excellent and the entry to Juan much better than that exhausting series of roundabouts and turns on the 'short cut'. During the early section of coast road the view back to old Antibes is exquisite.

Further on a right turn leads to **Jardin Thuret**, a large botanical garden named for its creator, Gustave Thuret. In the mid-nineteenth century Thuret imported plants from

Château Grimaldi was built in the twelfth century on Roman founda
tions, then rebuilt in the sixteenth century. It was then the home of the
Grimaldi family for a century. The castle houses an archaeological collection of
locally found Roman remains, but is chiefly memorable for its Picasso Museum.

Picasso spent six months working at the castle in 1946, donating the phenomenal output of work the period yielded to the town. The collection is fantastic,
truly illustrating Picasso's genius. Everyone will have a best liked work, but by
common consent *La Joie de Vivre* (The Joy of Life), a vast work on asbestos-
cement, is one of his masterpieces.

The castle also houses the Nicholas de Staël collection, the tortured canvases of
the Russian artist, born in St Petersburg in 1914, who committed suicide in
Antibes in 1955. There is also a collection of work of contemporary artists,
including some surprising and amusing sculptures, on a terrace above the sea.

La Joie de Vivre (The Joy of Life) Picasso Museum, Antibes

tropical climates, including the first eucalyptus from Australia, to study plant acclimatisation. The garden now has over 3,000 species of plants and trees, and is still a place of research.

To the east of the garden is the Plateau de la Garoupe. Here stands a lighthouse with one of the most powerful beams on the Riviera coast, carrying over 40 miles (60km), and a church well-known for its collection of sailors' *ex-voti*. The most famous piece is the Notre-Dame de Bon Port, Our Lady of Safe Homecoming, a gilded wooden statue of the patron saint of sailors.

Just past the actual *cap* is the **Musée Naval et Napoléonien** housed in the Le Grillon battery. The Napoleonic memorabilia includes his autograph, several proclamations, model soldiers from the Grand Army and a bust by Canova. The naval section includes many fine model ships.

JUAN-LES-PINS

The coast road now reaches Juan-les-Pins. Until the 1920s the Riviera was a winter resort, but after insecticides had eliminated the mosquitoes and refrigeration had allowed drinks to be kept cool it became possible to survive the summer.

The first to come were the Americans, Frank Jay Gould converting what was then the nondescript village of Juan to the hub of 20s social life for the rich and famous. Isadora Duncan, Douglas Fairbanks, Dorothy Parker, Mary Pickford, Cole Porter and Gertrude Stein all came, though the most famous of all the visitors were Scott and Zelda Fitzgerald.

The Americans brought jazz with them, this 'new' music becoming the spirit of the age. One of Fitzgerald's finest books, *Tender is the Night*, immortalizes the era.

Today Juan is a lively place during the week-long summer Jazz Festival, but to be fair it is a lively place at most other times too.

The Juan-les-Pins Jazz Festival

After the 1939-45 War Juan's reputation for jazz was revived by the French artist Sidney Bechet who was married in the town in 1951. Although there was no festival as such, Bechet played most summers until his death in 1959. After that the festival became a programmed, regular event and is now regarded as one of the world's premier jazz festivals. All the great jazz players of the both the pre- and post-War eras have played here: Louis Armstrong, Miles Davis, Duke Ellington, Dizzy Gillespie, and the finest musicians still come.

The festival is held outdoor with a temporary stage set among the pines at the *Cap d'Antibes* end of town. To sit among the rustling pines, with the Mediterranean just yards away and the stars overhead adds makes any concert here an incomparable experience.

Posters for the Juan Jazz Festival become collectors' items

Château Grimaldi and old Antibes from the beach

ON TO VALLAURIS

Continuing along the coast road, the visitor passes **Golfe-Juan**, where Napoleon landed after his escape from Elba. Napoleon ate at a local inn while his lieutenants negotiated with the Antibes garrison. The negotiations failed and the Emperor marched towards Cannes: despite this inauspicious start Napoleon reached Paris in triumph, though the triumph was to be short-lived.

Inland from the coast is **Vallauris**, the last place of note before Cannes is reached. In the town is the **National Picasso Museum**, built around his *War and Peace*, housed in the Romanesque chapel that is all that remains of a priory that originally stood on the site now occupied by the fine Renaissance castle. Picasso's mural, covering 150sq yd (125sq m),

was painted on plywood between 1952 and 1959. With its echoes of *Guernica*, its images re-state the horrors of war.

The castle, one of the few examples of Renaissance architecture in Provence, also houses a gallery of modern and contemporary art, the collections including two rooms of ceramics by Picasso and many works by the Florentine artist Alberto Magnelli. The ceramics are especially appropriate as Vallauris was once a thriving pottery town. Picasso's work revived the industry which is now flourishing again, with several workshops operating in the town: some of these can be visited to see the craftsmen at work. **The Musée de la Poterie** (Pottery Museum) in Rue Sicard, in a still-functioning workshop, explores the trade's history and techniques.

* = Closed on Official Holidays

Antibes

Jardin Thuret *
Cap d'Antibes
Open: All year, Monday to Friday
8am-6pm (5pm from October to
April). ☎ 93 67 88 86

Musée d'Archéologie *
Bastion St André
Open: All year, daily except Monday
10am-12noon, 2-6pm.
☎ 92 90 54 35

**Musée des Art
et Traditions Populaires**
2 Rue de l'Orme
Open: All year, April to September
Wednesday, Thursday and Saturday
4-7pm; October to March Wednesday, Thursday and Saturday 3-5pm.
☎ 93 34 50 91

Musée Naval et Napoléonien
Batterie du Grillon
Avenue John F Kennedy
Cap d'Antibes
Open: All year (except October),
Monday to Friday 9.30am-12noon,
2.15-6pm, Saturday 9.30am-
12noon.
☎ 93 61 45 32

Musée Peynet *
Place Nationale
Open: All year, daily except Monday
10am-12noon, 2-6pm.
☎ 92 90 54 29

Musée Picasso *
Château Grimaldi
Open: All year, June to September
daily except Monday 10am-6pm;
October to May daily except
Monday 10am-12noon, 2-6pm
☎ 92 90 54 20

Biot

Écomusée du Verre
(Glass Museum/Works)
Chemin des Combes
Open: All year, Monday to Saturday
9am-7pm, Sunday 10.30am-1pm,
2.30-7pm. ☎ 93 65 03 00

Marineland Complex
Marineland
On the N7 2.5 miles (4km)
north of Antibes
Open: All year, daily 10am-6pm
(10pm in July and August).
☎ 93 33 49 49

**Musée d'Histoire
et de Céramique de Biot**
9 Rue St Sébastien
Open: All year (except mid-
November to mid-December), May
to September daily except Monday
and Tuesday 2.30-6.30pm; October
to April daily except Monday and
Tuesday 2-6pm. ☎ 93 65 54 54

Musée National Fernand Léger
Signposted off the D4 south-east
of the village
Open: All year, June to September
daily except Tuesday 11am-6pm;
October to May daily except
Tuesday 10am-12.30pm,
2-5.30pm. ☎ 92 91 50 30

Cagnes-sur-Mer

Château Musée
Haut-de-Cagnes
Place Grimaldi
Open: All year (except mid-October
to mid-November), July to September daily except Tuesday 10am-
12.30pm, 1.30-6pm; all other
times daily except Tuesday
10am-12noon, 2-5pm.
☎ 93 20 87 29

Musée Renoir *
La Maison de Renoir
'Les Collettes'
Avenue des Collettes
Open: All year (except mid-October
to mid-November), May to September daily except Tuesday 10.30am-
12.30pm, 1.30-6pm; all other
times daily except Tuesday 10am-
12noon, 2-5pm (Gardens 10am-
5pm). ☎ 93 20 61 07

St Paul

Fondation Maeght
Route Passe-Prest
Open: All year, July to September
daily 10am-7pm; October to June
daily 10am-12.30pm, 2.30-6pm.
☎ 93 32 81 63

Musée d'Historie Locale

Place de l'Eglise (beside the church and town hall)
Open: All year, June to September daily 11am-6pm; October to May Saturday and Sunday 11am-6pm.
☎ 93 32 41 13

Vallauris

Château-Musée de Vallauris *

(National Picasso Museum/Modern Art Museum/Magnelli Collection)
Place de la Libération
Open: All year, daily except Tuesday 10am-12noon, 2-6pm; 10am-12.30pm, 2-6.30pm in July and August. ☎ 93 64 16 05

Musée de la Poterie

(Pottery Museum)
Rue Sicard
Open: All year (except January), daily 9am-12noon, 2-6pm.
☎ 93 64 66 51

Above: Old Antibes from Porte Marine Below: Fort Carré and the Harbour from Porte Marine, Antibes

Vence

Chapelle du Rosaire

Avenue Henri Matisse
Open: All year (except November to mid-December), Tuesday and Thursday 10-11.30am, 2.30-5.30pm; at other times by prior appointment. ☎ 93 58 03 26

Fondation Emile Hugues

Château des Villeneuve
Place du Frêne
Open: All year, July to October daily except Monday 10am-6pm; November to June daily except Monday 10am-12.30pm, 2-6pm.
☎ 93 58 15 78

Villeneuve-Loubet

Musée d'Art Culinaire *

(Fondation Auguste Escoffier)
3 Rue Escoffier
Open: All year, daily except Monday 2-6pm; 7pm from June to September. ☎ 93 20 80 51

Musée Militaire *

Place de Verdun
Open: All year, Monday to Friday 10am-12noon, 2-5pm, Saturday and Sunday 2-5pm.
☎ 93 02 60 39

3 Cannes

HISTORY

The Ligureans had a settlement at Cannes, probably on the hill of Le Suquet where later the Romans built a fort. Then in the eleventh century the Count of Provence gave the area to the monks on the island of Lérins. The monks built a tower at Le Suquet to protect the fisherfolk who were now the only inhabitants of Cannes. The monks could give an early warning of the approach of marauding Saracens or pirates and the families on the mainland could retreat into the tower for safety. The tower was entered by a door at first floor level: when everyone was inside, they pulled up the ladder and left the attackers scratching their heads at the base. When long term peace eventually came, Le Suquet lost its strategic importance and Cannes became a quiet fishing port. Then came 1834 and the development of the new town of Cannes beneath the old town by Lord Brougham and his compatriots.

It is the new town that visitors come to see: Le Suquet and old Cannes is quaint and the views from it are splendid, but the glamour lies at its foot.

Boulevard de la Croisette

To the east of Le Suquet and the Old Town is an endless sandy beach and the glittering Boulevard de la Croisette – the essence of modern Cannes which no one should miss – with hotels, shops, cafés and marinas. As appropriate a starting point as could be imagined for an exploration of

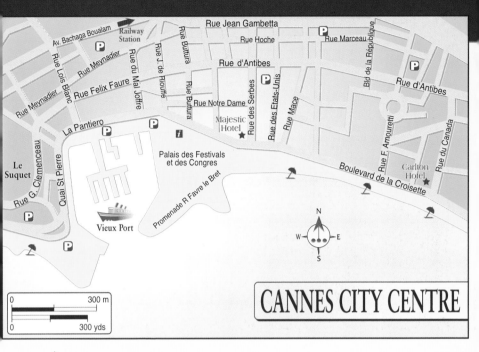

CANNES CITY CENTRE

Lord Brougham and Cannes

In 1834 Henry, Lord Brougham, the British Lord Chancellor, visited the south of France to take a holiday. He was exhausted by years of parliamentary service which had included a leading role in the abolition of slavery and concerned for the health of his daughter, Eleonore who accompanied him.

The pair arrived at the border between France and Sardinian Savoy – the River Var, close to where the airport now stands to the west of Nice – in a coach drawn by six horses rather than in a *brougham*, the four-wheeled, one-horse-drawn coach that his lordship had invented. The Savoyans refused them entry as there was a cholera epidemic in Provence and they did not have the necessary papers to prove they had undergone quarantine. Brougham tried to get rooms in an inn at Antibes, but it was full, so he returned to a hotel near the small fishing village of *Canois,* named for the reeds that grew in the Harbour.

Brougham was enchanted with the village: within a week he had bought a plot of land on which he had a villa built. Villa Eleonore was ready in 1838 and Brougham spent all his winters there from that time(another 34 of them: he was almost 90 when he died), persuading many friends to join him.

Some idea of the lifestyle and wealth of these early British residents of Cannes can be gained from the fact that each winter they arrived with turfs cut in Britain which were used to returf their lawns, British grass not surviving the Mediterranean summers.

Cannes is **Palais des Festivals et des Congrès** at the western, Old Town, end of the Croisette (as the sea-front boulevard is known locally), the home of the famous film festival, amongst many others.

• THE CANNES FILM FESTIVAL •

The Festival was first held in September 1946, part of the effort to add a little glamour to the austerity of post-war France, but only really became an international event in the 1950s when Hollywood film moguls conceived that it was a good showcase for their new films (and was, therefore, a complete contrast to the Oscars ceremony which only celebrated old films). From 1952 the Festival has been held in May.

As the importance of the Festival increased so did the budget for the promotional stunts for the films: during the party to celebrate the screening of *Never on Sunday* several thousand champagne glasses were smashed in typical Greek fashion. The stunts of the wannabe starlets also increased, the hordes of photographers never tiring of scantily clad young ladies trying (and succeeding) to attract attention to themselves on the Croisette and the beach.

The main events of the Festival are now held in the Palais des Festivals et des Congrès opened in 1982. It is known locally as 'The Bunker', a term usually claimed to be affectionate, but one which most architectural critics agree with when speaking in less complimentary terms.

It is around the Bunker that the crowds stand each May hoping to catch just a glimpse of the stars as they attempt to outdo each other in the opulence and style of their event-wear. Some stars love the place, others hate it: Dirk Bogarde famously claimed that he never went to Cannes because he knew he would find it full of people he had secretly hoped were dead.

The Palais des Festivals

Around the Palais is the *Allée des Stars*, the chain of hand prints of the famous in the cement paving slabs. It is as close as most mere mortals will ever come to the celebrities.

Beside the Palais there is a small piece of parkland with a large carousel and the Croisette starts in earnest. The Cannes beach is almost wholly taken over by private operators, many attached to the hotels on the other side of the road, public areas being smaller and harder to find than at Nice, which is sad because the beach is actually a better one for sunbathing.

The main public beaches are at the eastern end – towards and around the Pointe Croisette, the headland which names the famous Boulevard and is itself named for an ancient cross which stands on it – and to the west, beyond Le Suquet where Boulevard Midi, which links Cannes with La Napoule is hemmed in by the railway on one side and miles of sunworshippers on the other. Cars can be parked on the seaward side of this road – come early to avoid the disappointment of a long, difficult drive and a mad scramble for a space which, inevitably, will be both too small and the object of someone else's desire.

As with Promenade des Anglais, the Croisette offers daylong entertainment to both purposeful walkers and strolling on-lookers. There is a regular fashion parade by the youthful holidaymakers and the young of Cannes, exhibitions by roller-bladers slaloming along lines of cola cans, artists offering their work, and the parasailors, water-skiers and others on the sea.

Glamorous hotels

Across the Croisette, seen through the pines and palm trees that add yet another elegant touch to the street, are the famous Cannes hotels and an array of classy shops. The Majestic where the bathrooms are marble; the Noga Hilton, built on the site of the original Festival palace and with a staircase to the main door which has enhanced many a publicity shot; the Carlton; and the Martinez, built in the 1920s and now arguably the grandest place in town after a period of decline. Though renovated, the Martinez still has memories of its Art Deco beginnings. **La Malmaison** at No. 47, once an annex of the Grand Hotel, is now an art exhibition complex with a regular schedule of temporary shows.

The Carlton Hotel and La Belle Otéro

The Carlton was built in 1912 by the Swiss hotelier Henri Ruhl. Ruhl was captivated by Caroline Otéro, a beautiful half-gypsy girl who made a small living as an actress and a very much larger one as a 'paramour' (to use the somewhat demure expression of the time).

La Belle Otéro, as she was known, had kept company with kings and was both rich and famous and had no intention of becoming a hotelier's wife despite Ruhl's long and desperate entreaties. The rejected and depressed Ruhl is said to have modelled the hotel's cupolas on his part-time lover's most prominent features! The hotel's fine restaurant is today called La Belle Otéro.

Le Suquet

Cannes' old port lies beside the Palais des Festivals. It is fronted by La Pantiéro which also encloses one side of the Allées de la Liberté, a popular tree-shaded open area. Here each morning there is a flower market and there are regular flea markets. Under the shade of the trees boule players can be found most times of day, the gentle clink of the balls a complete contrast to the bustle on the Croisette. All these activities are watched over by a statue of Lord Brougham raised by a grateful population. The verse on the statue's base is by Stephen Liégard, the man credited with creating the name Côte d'Azur.

The Old Town of Cannes, smaller than that at Nice, but no less interesting, occupies rising ground above the port and is dominated by the **Tour Le Suquet**, the beacon which identifies it from a distance. Not surprisingly, there is a fine view from the top for all who climb the 70ft (21m) Chevalier Tower, though the view from the nearby terrace is almost as good.

Near the tower, which houses temporary photographic exhibitions during the summer months, is the **Musée Le Castre**, with fine collections of antiquities from all over the world donated by a Dutch baron in the 1870s. After admiring the view from close to the tower, be sure to see the church of ND de l'Espérance (Our Lady of Good Hope) a lovely little sixteenth century church in Provençal Gothic style. Inside there are several medieval carvings.

INLAND CANNES

Le Suquet and the seafront is most of Cannes, but not all of it. Shoppers will head inland to Rue d'Antibes and those who wish to see where the famous lived and where the rich residents still live can drive through the villas of Croix des Gardes and La Californie. Lord Brougham's Villa Eleonore is at 24 Avenue du Dr Picaud on the lower slopes of the hill of Croix des Gardes, the first residential area of holiday resort Cannes. La Californie lies on the other, eastern, side of the town, inland from Pointe Croisette. The British already having claimed Croix des Gardes, it was first settled by Russians, who built villas in a variety of styles, some of them quite fantastic, and later by the Americans (whose presence named the area).

Sadly, none of the villas are open to the public, though the only non-museum in Cannes which is open lies on the town side of La Californie, in Avenue de Vallauris. Here, **Chapelle Bellini**, built in Florentine Baroque style in the 1890s by Count Vitali can be visited. The chapel stands in the quiet, pretty Parc Fiorentina and was for 30 years the studio of the artist E Bellini who worked in Murano glass and produced jewelry but is best known for his paintings of the Croisette which capture the spirit of the pre-War years. The studio is now used by his daughter, Lucette, who is also an artist.

Finally, head north of the old port, taking the wide Boulevard Carnot to Le Cannet, now a suburb of the larger town, but famous as the home of the painter Pierre Bonnard. The **St Saveur Chapel**, in the road of the

As might be expected for a town inundated with the stars of Hollywood on a regular basis, Cannes is a shoppers' paradise. Most of the shopping is also concentrated in just two streets, which makes it even easier. Boulevard de la Croisette tends to have the really expensive shops, while Rue d'Antibes, running more or less parallel to it, but one street back, is for mere mortals.

Chanel, Christian Dior, Escada, Hermès and Yves St Laurent are all on the Croisette, as is Louis Vuitton for those looking for leather. Alexandra, which sells the creations of Christian Lacroix, Ungaro, Givenchy and others can be found on the Rond-Point Duboys d'Angers the really lovely little circular 'square' between the Croisette and Rue d'Antibes (follow Rue Amouretti along the side of the Noga Hilton).

For jewelry, Bulgari are also there – in the Hôtel Majestic – as is Van Cleef & Arpels. Louis Julian, which sell major names in jewelry and also some of its own designs can be found in Rue d'Antibes. Rue d'Antibes also has Escada Sport and Max Mara and some really excellent shops of local designers.

Rue d'Antibes is also where visitors will find souvenirs and excellent wine, olive oil and confectionery shops.

There is a flower market every day, except Mondays in winter, at Allées de la Liberté opposite the old port, and regular flea markets are held there too. Place Gambetta, just a short step from Rue d'Antibes (head north from the old town side of the Grand Hôtel) has a daily fruit and vegetable market and a daily flea market as well.

Window-shopping on Boulevard de la Croisette

same name, has been redecorated by the artist Tobiasse, and is worth visiting for its wooden panelling, stained glass windows and the Murano enamel mosaic of the Creation of the World on the external façade. In the same road (Rue St-Saveur), at No. 190 is another external artwork, a fresco of the famous lovers of Raymond Peynet.

Iles de Lérins

From the old port, beneath Le Suquet, boats leave for the islands that dominate the Bay of Cannes, reaching the Ile Ste Marguerite in 15 minutes, Ile St Honorat in 25. (As an aside, boats also leave from here to St Tropez, taking about 1 hour 15 minutes and offering a fabulous view of the Esterel Mountains and the coast.)

Sightseeing of the historical buildings on the two islands combines with walks through pine and eucalyptus woodlands to make this an attractive half-day excursion. St Honorat is named for the fourth century saint who retreated to the island and was later joined by disciples who built the first monastery. The island became a famous pilgrimage site, pilgrims walking around it barefoot as a penance, though its holiness did not protect it from attacks by Saracens and pirates: the fortifications necessary to protect churches in the early medieval period can be gauged from the fortifications around the eleventh century abbey.

The **ruins** include arcaded cloisters and offer lovely views of the islands and the mainland. Later military occupation reduced the number of monks who found that weaponry and the canonical round were not compatible. The monastery was closed during the Revolution, but monks

Chapelle Bellini
Parc Fiorentina
67bis Avenue de Vallauris
Open: All year, Monday to Friday
2-5pm; 6pm from June-September.
☎ 93 38 61 80

Chapelle St Sauveur
(Musée Tobiasse)
74 Rue St Saveur
Le Cannet
Open: All year, daily except
Tuesday and Thursday 2-6pm.
☎ 93 45 34 27

La Malmaison
47 Boulevard de la Croisette
Open: All year; opening times depend upon exhibition but are generally daily except Tuesday 10am-5pm.
☎ 93 99 04 04

came to the island again in the 1850s: it is now the home of Cistercian monks who occupy a nineteenth century **monastery** which incorporates some older sections. The monks farm some of the island, though most of it is covered by a beautiful pine forest, and distil a potent liqueur.

Ste Marguerite

The larger island, Ste Marguerite, is largely covered with eucalyptus and pine forest through which broad paths cut. The northern side is dominated by the Royal Fort, built by Cardinal Richelieu and reinforced by Vauban, the greatest of military architects. Within the Fort are the **Musée de la Mer** (Naval Museum), partially housed in rooms built by the Romans, and the prison cells. The museum has a collection of archaeological finds, some of them discovered beneath the sea in the Bay, but most visitors are more interested in the cell of the Man in the Iron Mask.

Musée de la Castre
Château de la Castre
Le Suquet
Open: All year (except January),
April to June daily except Tuesday
10am-12noon, 2-6pm; July to
September daily except Tuesday
10am-12noon, 3-7pm; October
to March daily except Tuesday
10am-12noon, 2-5pm.
☎ 93 38 55 26

Monastère de St Honorat
Ile de St Honorat
Open: All year, daily except Sunday
morning 8.30-11.15am, 2-4.30pm.
Closed on public holidays.
☎ 93 48 68 68

Ruins of ancient fort
Ile de St Honorat
Open: All year, July and August
daily except Sunday
morning 10am-12noon,
2.30-4.30pm; September to
June daily except Sunday morning
9am-4pm. Closed on public
holidays.
☎ 93 48 68 68

Musée de la Mer
Ile Ste Marguerite (in the enclosure
of the Royal Fortress)
Open: All year, July to September
daily 10.30am-12.15pm and 2.15-
6pm; April to June daily 10.30am-
12.15pm, 2.15-5.30pm; October to
March daily 10.30am-12.15pm,
2.15-4pm.
☎ 93 43 18 17

RESTAURANTS IN CANNES

The most famous, and one of the most expensive restaurants in the town is **La Belle Otéro** in the Hôtel Carlton, named for the inspirational lover of the hotel's builder. The **Palme d'Or** in the Hôtel Martinez is of similar quality.

For very good cooking at more affordable prices try:

La Cave (FF)
9 Boulevard de la République
☎ 93 99 79 87
A traditionally furnished restaurant with a Provençal menu posted on a blackboard.

L' Auberge Provençale (FF)
Rue St Antoine, ☎ 92 99 27 17
Claimed to be the oldest restaurant in Le Suquet. Traditional regional cooking in a friendly atmosphere.

Gaston-Gastounette (FF)
6-7 Quai St Pierre, ☎ 93 39 47 92
Overlooking the old port. Traditional regional menu.

Chez Astoux (F)
43 Rue Félix Faure, ☎ 93 39 06 22
Seafood restaurant close to the Allées de la Liberté.

Caveau 30 (F)
45 Rue Félix Faure, ☎ 93 39 06 33
A good alternative to the above as it is next door! Excellent brasserie.

For a cup of coffee most visitors are looking for somewhere on the elegant Croisette. Be careful, some of the cafés there can be pricey. One that is not is:

Le Voilier
61 Boulevard de la Croisette
☎ 93 94 26 82

At the base of the Le Suquet hill there is a quiet square from which steps lead up into the old town. There, try:

Bar du Port
2 Rue de la Rampe
☎ 92 98 82 40

NORTH TO GRASSE

North of Cannes the N85 follows the Route Napoléon crossing the autoroute close to the **Musée de l'Automobile** which can, appropriately, also be entered from a service area on the motorway (either eastbound or westbound). The museum has a collection of over 200 cars, both production and racing models.

At **Mougins** the church tower can be climbed for a tremendous view. The town also has a photographic museum with a collection of cameras, prints from some of the world's most famous photographers and a collection of portraits of Picasso by the world's leading portraitists. A second museum (Musée Municipal) deals with the history of the town.

Route Napoléon

R oute Napoléon is the one followed by Napoleon on his march to Paris after his landing in Golfe Juan from Elba. It is marked by signs with the symbol of a flying eagle clutching a wreathed N, recalling the Emperor's famous proclamation which stated that 'the eagle... will fly from steeple to steeple until he reaches the towers of Notre-Dame'. Napoleon's aides had warned him against following the Rhône valley as the local commanders there were hostile and so moved north directly from the coast.

Beyond Mougins is **Mouans-Sartoux**, a charming little village. The old castle has been turned into a museum of contemporary art. Ahead now is Grasse, but a short detour eastwards (to the right) crosses the lovely Valbonne plateau where pines and holm oak grow. At **Valbonne**, a straggling place, there is an interesting museum which explores the plateau's arts and traditions.

Grasse

A town of great charm, Grasse spreads out over shallow hills as though relaxing in the sun or, perhaps, guarding the perfume meadows that have made it famous. In the very early Middle Ages the town was a republic, despite its size, with links to the Italian city-state of Pisa. The bigger state of Provence soon put an end to this independence of spirit.

Several centuries later the town lay virtually on Napoleon's route north after his landing at Antibes. The Emperor, fearful of the reception he might receive, went round the town, only staying locally for an hour to rest his men on what is now known as Napoleon's Plateau. Today Grasse is one of the top of the French perfume industries, with fields of perfume-bearing flowers all around the town.

The best place to start exploring is Place du Cours, a terraced promenade set above an underground car park that is the most convenient for visitors. From the Place there are fine views over the Old Town, to the east. The fountain dates from the time of the Revolution, while the statue commemorates the artist Jean-Honoré Fragonard, the great Provençal artist who was born in the town in 1732. The artist's name lives on in one of the town's three big perfumeries, that originally set up in his villa.

At the eastern (town) end of Place du Cours steps lead down: bear slightly left to reach the **Musée International de la Perfumerie** with its collection of items on the history of the industry. The collection of perfume bottles and flasks is especially interesting as are the buildings which house them, as they date from distinct periods of French architecture.

Beside the museum is another, the **Musée Amiral de Grasse**, a naval museum, named for a French admiral who was active in the American War of Independence. De Grasse was born at nearby Bar-sur-Loup and has a vessel of the French Navy named for him. The museum includes a fine collection of model ships of the Admiral's time.

In Rue Jean Ossola on the other side of the Perfume Museum in the Hôtel de Clapiers-Cabris, a fine seventeenth century mansion, there is a museum of Provençal costume and jewelry with some exceptional pieces of antique jewelry.

To the right from the bottom of Place du Cours steps is the **Villa-Musée Fragonard**. The museum has six rooms dedicated to the history of the perfume industry set above one of the company's perfume factories. Guided tours of the factory explain the perfume-making process and conclude with a visit to the site shop.

For reasons of copyright Fragonard (or the similar factories of Molinard and Galimard) cannot sell the perfumes of the big perfume houses by name – but can offer much the same product under a different name, and cheaper. The two other large perfumeries in the town, Molinard and Galimard, also have factory outlets which can be visited.

The **Fragonard Museum** stands at the corner of Rue Mirabeau. Turn down this to reach the **Musée d'Art et d'Histoire de Provence** with its collection of furniture, ceramics (including Moustiers ware), coins and items of local archaeology. In the basement is a reconstructed

Santons

During the Revolution, when churches were closed, Jean-Louis Lagnel, a Marseille sculpture, started to make small figures that the locals, deprived of access to their nativities at Christmas, could use to create their own cribs. The figures, formed in clay, fired and painted in bright tones, were called *santons*, 'little saints' in Provençal. Their appeal was immediate and santon cribs soon become an important feature of Provençal homes. When churches re-opened, santon cribs were often set up within them, the santon makers turning their hands to more traditional figures – knife grinders, fishermen, milkmaids and so on. Today santon making is one of the Provence's most traditional crafts, the figurines being one of the area's best loved souvenirs.

To create a perfume it is first necessary to extract an essence. Chiefly, and always in the early days of the industry, these essences are derived from flowers. Initially the extraction was carried out by placing the flowers individually on blocks of animal fat, the fat absorbing the essence over a period of weeks and then giving it up when the fat was combined with the fixing agents. Today, steam extraction is used to reduce the time and expense of the process.

The end-product of the extraction process is pure essence. It takes 660lb (300kg) of lavender to produce 2.2lb (1kg) of lavender essence, the figure rising to 1,325lb (600kg) for rose and to 2,200lb (1,000kg) for some of the more exotic essences.

The next stage in the process is for the factory's 'nose' to blend the essences to form a unique aroma. The factories in Grasse work for the big perfume houses of Paris and other big-name houses of the fashion world. The houses specify the type of perfume they wish to have created – a lively one for young wearers, an exciting fragrance for evening wear and so on – and the 'nose' creates the aroma for them. The 'noses' cannot smoke or eat spicy food and must drink alcohol in moderation or their skill – for which they are very well paid – will be destroyed. No one who cannot distinguish at least 500 individual essences can hope to become a 'nose', and the very best can easily distinguish as many as 4,500.

Once the fragrance has been agreed, it is distilled into alcohol. *Eau de Parfum* contains 20 per cent essence in 80 per cent alcohol. For an *Eau de Toilette*, the ingredients are 10 per cent essence, 10 per cent distilled water and 80 per cent alcohol.

The best of the fragrances created by the 'noses' – and the ones which therefore cost the

Left: The Palais des Congres, Grasse

Above: The shop at the Fragonard Perfumery

eighteenth century kitchen and a superb collection of cribs and *santons*.

Bear left at the bottom of Rue Mirabeau to reach the **Tour de Guet**, once the Bishop's Palace and now the Town Hall, the name deriving from the huge, twelfth-century square tower. Close by is the cathedral, renovated in the seventeenth century in Provençal Gothic style. Inside are three paintings by Rubens given to the cathedral by a town resident. To the north of the cathedral is the **Old Town**, an area of tight streets and alleys that is well worth exploring: be sure to find the Place aux Aires with its tiered fountain and arcaded houses.

THE VALLEY OF THE LOUP

From Grasse a short journey east reaches the valley of the Loup with a delightful series of villages and a superb gorge.

Gourdon is the best of the villages, standing above the river and with spectacular views of it, and of the Esterel, from the square beside the church and the old castle. The castle, built in the thirteenth century on the ruins of a Saracen fortress and newly restored, includes a history and art museum. The history section has a good collection of weapons, sixteenth century furniture and a self-portrait by Rembrandt. The art collection is of naïve work from the period 1925-70, and is one of the best in southern France.

Just beyond the turn to Gourdon is one to the Gorge du Loup, an impressive, tight gorge, its road narrow enough to cause the driver problems on busy days. Not far along the gorge is the 130ft (40m) Courmes

most – are actually a mixture of aromas. The essences are very volatile and as they disappear the fragrance changes subtly. In general, the very best perfumes will have three distinct aromas, the first lasting around an hour, the second about 6 hours and the last as long as 24 hours. In the trade these are known as the head, the heart and the body, for fairly obvious (and basic) reasons.

One final trade secret – fragrances kept in glass will lose their aroma in time as the essence reacts with the glass. The big perfume houses always use glass because more attractive containers can be made with it. For the very best long-term storage it is essential to use aluminum containers which are non-reacting. The *parfumeries* of Grasse invariably sell in aluminum.

waterfall – drive past, through the tunnel and park tidily on the roadside beyond. In summer there are often children here, playing in the pool below the fall, which cascades away from the overhanging rock. Further on, at an incongruous bar/café/kiosk, the visitor can pay a small fee to see the **Saut du Loup**, a huge pothole scrapped out by glacial and river action.

From the gorge a narrow road can be followed to **Tourette-sur-Loup**, originally a Ligurean settlement but named by the Romans for an observation post (*turres altae*) they maintained to keep an eye an the hill tribes. After the Revolution it gradually emptied of people, but was rediscovered by artists after World War II. Today it is a flourishing art and craft village, almost every house given over to artwork, from hand-painted T-shirts to sculpture. From Tourettes it is a short drive to Vence, a return to Cannes then being made by heading south to the A8 to complete an excellent circular tour.

THE VERDON GORGE

From Cannes a very long day trip takes the A8 westwards, exiting for Draguinan from where the D557 to Aups and then the D957 northwards reaches Moustiers-Ste-Marie and the Verdon Gorge. Though long, the day is really worthwhile, the Gorge being one of the wonders of Europe and Moustiers being a lovely little place with a fascinating history.

The Gorge was formed by the Verdon River, a tributary of the Durance, cutting into the limestone plateau over which it flowed. The production of such deep, clean cut gorges is not well-understood, but whatever the exact nature of the process, the result is clear, with the river now hemmed in by narrow cliffs which plunge 2,300ft (700m) amid wild scenery.

The Verdon gets its name from its green jade waters which add to the beauty. On both sides of the Gorge there are excellent viewpoints, both of the majestic cliffs and, occasionally, of the rock climbers at work on them.

Moustiers-Ste Marie

Set at the western end of the Gorge's Grand Canyon, Moustiers-Ste Marie is famous for its pottery – reputedly introduced to the town by a monk from Faenza in Italy in medieval times, but refined over many centuries by French artists and craftsmen. The town has many shops selling modern Moustiers-ware, but equally fascinating is the **Musée de la Faïence** (Pottery Museum) where the history and development of the local work is shown through numerous examples.

The village is beautifully positioned at the base of a narrow ravine, its huge, almost vertical, walls dominating the main village square. From the square a steep path leads to the twelfth century church of Notre-Dame du Beauvoir from where there are dramatic views of the village, the ravine and the Verdon Gorge. High above is a star suspended from a rusty chain strung across the ravine. The original is said to have been erected in the thirteenth century by Baron Blacas d'Auls, a local lord, to celebrate his release from captivity after one of the Crusades. The present star dates from 1957.

For those with the time, Sentier Martel – named for Édouard-Alfred Martel, the first man to travel along its length, a journey which took almost 4 days – is a fantastic walk. The walk takes about half a day and walkers should be well-equipped, with boots, warm and waterproof clothing (as there is no escape once the route has been started), food and water, especially in summer when the Gorge is a sun trap and the river is usually too difficult to reach. Head torches must be carried as the route uses tunnels through the rock in several places. There are also ladders to be descended (or climbed) and some exposed sections of paths. But with those provisos, the walk – which links La Malene with Point Sublime – is a truly unforgettable experience. If you are planning to complete it, please obtain a copy of the local map and, if possible, a guide book.

Above: Pleasure craft on the Verdon river
Below: Admiring the view from Point Sublime

Gourdon

Château du Gourdon (Museum of Naïve and Medieval Art)
Open: June to September daily 11am-1pm, 2-7pm, ☎ 93 09 68 02

Grasse

Musée d'Art et d'Histoire de Provence
2 rue Mirabeau
Open: All year (except November), June to September daily 10am-7pm; October, December to May Wednesday to Sunday 10am-12pm, 2-5pm. Closed on official holidays. ☎ 93 36 01 61

Musée du Costume et du Bijou
Hôtel de Clapiers-Cabris, 2 Rue Jean Ossola
Open: Easter to October daily 10am-1pm, 2-6pm. ☎ 93 36 44 65

Musée Jean-Honoré Fragonard
23 Boulevard Fragonard
Open: All year (except November), June to September daily 10am-7pm; October, December to May Wednesday to Sunday 10am-12noon, 2-5pm. Closed on official holidays. ☎ 93 36 01 61

Musée International de la Parfumerie
8 place du Cours, Grasse
Open: All year (except November), June to September daily 10am-7pm; October, December to May Wednesday to Sunday 10am-12noon, 2-5pm. Closed on official holidays. ☎ 93 36 80 20

Musée de la Marine
2 Boulevard Jeu de Ballon
Open: All year (except November), June to September daily 10am-7pm; October, December to May daily except Sunday 10am-12noon, 2-6pm. Closed on official holidays. ☎ 93 40 11 11

Parfumerie Fragonard
Route de Cannes
Open: All year, May to September daily 9am-6.15pm; October to April daily 9am-12.30pm, 2-6pm. ☎ 93 36 44 65

Parfumerie Galimard
73 Route de Cannes
Open: All year, May to September daily 9am-6pm; October to April daily 9am-12noon, 2-6pm. ☎ 93 09 20 00

Parfumerie Molinard
60 Boulevard Victor Hugo
Open: All year, May to September daily 9am-7pm; October to April daily 9am-12.30pm, 2-6pm. ☎ 93 36 01 62

Boulevard de la Croisette from the Old Harbour, Cannes

Near the Old Harbour, Cannes

Musée Municipal
Place de la Mairie
Open: All year (except November),
Monday to Friday 10am-12noon,
2-6pm.
☎ 92 92 50 42

Musée de la Photographie
Porte Sarrazine
Mougins-Village
Open: All year (except November),
July and August daily except
Tuesday 2-11pm; other months
daily except Tuesday 1-6pm.
☎ 93 75 85 67

Moustiers-Ste Marie

Musée de la Faïence
Place du Presbytère
Open: April to October daily
(except Tuesday) 9am-12noon,
2-6pm. ☎ 94 74 61 64

Valbonne

Musée des Arts et Traditions Populaires
Abbaye de Valbonne,
Rue de la Paroisse
Open: All year, June to September
daily except Monday 3-7pm;
October to May daily except
Monday 2-6pm. ☎ 93 12 96 54

Villa-Musée Fragonard
20 Boulevard Fragonard
Open: All year (except November),
June to September daily 10am-
7pm; October, December to May
Wednesday to Sunday 10am-
12noon, 2-5pm. Closed on official
holidays. ☎ 93 36 44 65

Mouans-Sartoux

Château de Mouans
(Espace de l'Art Concret)
Open: All year, June to September
daily except Tuesday 11am-7pm;
October to May Thursday to Sunday
11am-6pm. ☎ 93 75 71 50

Mougins

Musée de l'Automobiliste
(Autoroute A8 Nice-Cannes,
Aire de Bréguieres)
Les Hautes Bréguirès
772 Chemin de Font-de-Currault
Open: All year, April to September
daily 10am-7pm; October to March
daily 10am-6pm. ☎ 93 69 27 80

The Palais des Festivals from the water front, Cannes

4

Heading west from Cannes the visitor passes the long public beach of the Golfe de la Napoule to reach La Napoule with its Harbour and massive medieval castle, of which only two huge fourteenth-century towers remain. These were restored by the American Henry Clews and are a museum of his sculptures. The castle's gardens are superb and are included in a castle tour. Inland from La Napoule is the town of Mandelieu with a pleasant array of shops, but chiefly memorable to most visitors for its exit/entrance to the A8 autoroute.

Beyond La Napoule the coast road goes through the neat coastal village of **Théoule-sur-Mer** then runs past a number of easily reached, but rarely visited coves. Parking beside the main road allows access to these: some are so remote that they are often used by naturists. Further on the visitor leaves the official Côte d'Azur, entering the *département* of Var.

Inland now is the Massif de l'Esterel, an ancient and eroded range whose highest peak, **Mont Vinaigre**, rises to only 2,060ft (628m). The peaks are of volcanic porphyry, whose jagged, rust-red rocks plunge dramatically into the ultramarine sea. Esterel is the most vivid part of the Riviera coast, less wooded than the Maures hills near St Tropez, but with areas of *maquis*, a dense, shrubby undergrowth comprising gorse, lavender, cistus and heather.

Squashed between the red peaks and the blue sea the N98, sometimes called the Corniche d'Or, passes through a number of small, little known resorts – Le Trayas, Anthéor, Agay – each with good beaches and adequate, if limited, facilities before reaching the major conurbation of **Fréjus-St Raphaël**.

FRÉJUS

Fréjus is far enough inland not to be a resort, its chief attractions being its Roman and medieval past. Two thousand years ago the town was on the sea and Caesar created a trading post here, *Forum Julii*, on the Aurelian Way, in 49BC. A little later, Octavius, the future Emperor Augustus, developed the place into a major naval base and settlement for his retired soldiers. For 200 years the large port was kept skillfully dredged but then its importance diminished, the River Argens silted it up, and Fréjus became surrounded by malarial marshes.

The remains of *Forum Julii* can be toured by taking a little train (the *train de soleil*) from Esplanade Vernet near the Cathedral Close. The best remains are Gaul's Gate, where one of the two original towers remains, the theatre and the arena. This was built in the second century AD and could accommodate 10,000. It is the oldest amphitheatre in Gaul but was not built to the high Roman standard seen in Roman Provence (at Arles and Nîmes). The seating has been restored – bullfights and concerts are held in the amphitheatre in summer.

In 1910 Fréjus became the site of the first air and sea base in France, and visitors interested in military history can visit several unusual sites. The **Musée des Troupes de Marine** is a museum of the French marines from the seventeenth century through to the present day.

More poignant is the memorial to the soldiers who died in France's Indochina campaign. The remains of more than 20,000 dead have been brought from Asia to the necropolis here. The Buddhist pagoda was built by the Vietnamese in homage to their comrades killed during the 1914-18 War, while the Mosque (a model of one in Mali) was built in the 1920s by Senegalese troops stationed at the Fréjus camp.

A short distance to the west of the town the Frejus **Zoo** has a small

The Cathedral Close, Fréjus

The Cathedral Close, the Episcopal area of medieval Fréjus, is comprised of a cathedral, cloisters, baptistery and bishop's palace, the whole being fortified. The austere, early Provençal Gothic cathedral is thirteenth century. When you enter, it is clear that it is powerful rather than graceful, Provençal architects not having yet mastered the subtlety of Gothic art. Make a point of seeing a retable on wood by the Nice painter Jacques Durandi (1450), and the fifteenth-century chancel choirstalls.

Close by is a fourth- or fifth-century baptistery, octagonal inside, and one of the oldest in France. In the restored thirteenth-century cloisters, a garden and ancient well are surrounded by delicate, twin-column marble pillars; the beams of the arcades were painted in the fourteenth and fifteenth centuries with innumerable creatures and grotesques illustrating the Apocalypse. Adjoining the cloisters is the Archaeological Museum with items from Roman Fréjus.

safari park (elephants, zebra etc) and a large collection of birds. The zoo is set in lovely parkland.

St Raphaël

St Raphaël is the beach-half of Fréjus, though to say so in the town would be to risk permanent injury. Like Fréjus, St Raphaël is of Roman origin, though it is better known for being at the heart of two incidents in the life of Napoleon. In 1799

Bonaparte landed here on his return from Egypt. Fifteen years later he departed from here on his way to exile on Elba. A pyramid in Cours Commandant Guilbaud, near the port, commemorates the earlier event, but no one remembers the later one.

Scuba-divers have helped fill the town's archaeology museum, amph-orae and other finds being housed there, together with a display on the techniques of underwater archaeology. Closer to the sea the church of St-Pierre-des-Templiers, built in the twelfth century in Provençal Romanesque style, is fortress-like, having been built to protect the townsfolk from sea-borne marauders.

ON TO STE-MAXIME

From Fréjus the N98 follows the coast in fine style, again sandwiched between hills and the sea. Here the hills are the Massif des Maures, built of crystalline schists. beyond Fréjus-Plage are lovely little resorts hidden among the trees, all with spectacular views – St Aygulf, Les Issambres, San Peire-sur-Mer, Val d'Esquières. Cap des Sardinaux, which the Maures thrusts into the sea, is yet another stopping-place for exhilarating views The road then rounds the Pointe des Sardinaux to reach Ste-Maxime.

Ste-Maxime is a fashionable and lively resort which is sheltered, unlike St Tropez across the bay, from the *mistral*. Fine beaches – especially at La Nartelle, entertainment at night and plenty of hotels and restaurants make it very popular. The town has a small local history museum housed in Dames Tower, built in the sixteenth century by the monks of

Port Grimaud

This museum, housed in a building that itself looks like a barrel-organ, has a strong claim to being the most unusual on the Riviera. It comprises a collection of over 300 instruments and music-making machines, with a collection of old gramophones, musical boxes and barrel organs and some very rare examples of the melophone (an early accordion) and pianola.

Lérins to defend the town, and an extraordinary museum of mechanical music.

PORT GRIMAUD

The N98 now continues close to the shore, with excellent views across the Golfe de St Tropez to the town itself. In summer this road can be packed with cars making progress slow and frustrating. If that is the case, take time out by visiting **Port Grimaud**.

You must leave the car at the entrance to the village, for Port Grimaud can be visited only on foot or by boat. It is an elegant, modern holiday village designed by François Spoerry and built out into the Golfe de St Tropez. It was designed with the yachting community in mind: each front door has its own mooring. In imitation of Provençal fishing villages it has harmonious tones and graceful bridges over canals from one walkway to another.

Shops, banks, cafés, church and post-office are grouped around a square which is decked with flowers. Self-drive boats can be rented to tour the canals, and there are sightseeing cruises.

ST TROPEZ

The French – and, taking their lead, most visitors – call the port St Trop: an endearing nickname, but it is as well to remember that *trop* in French means 'too much'. There is excess in St Tropez, the shops and restaurant are often too expensive, there are always too many cars and usually too many people. But once the yachts, aspirants to stardom or notoriety, naturists and the crowds who want to share in the dream-world have left, St Tropez reveals itself to be as endearingly attractive as it was when Matisse painted it long ago.

The scenic quay at St Tropez has attracted artists for decades

Matisse followed Paul Signac whose boat was forced into the port by bad weather. Signac like St Tropez so much he built a villa and stayed. He also spread word of the town's charms: soon Matisse, Derain, Braque, Marquet, Bonnard, Dufy and a host of other artists fell under the spell of the white light and immortalized St Tropez in paint, as did Colette in literature.

The work of some of these turn-of-the century masters is housed in the **Annunciation Museum** housed in the sixteenth century chapel of Notre-Dame d'Annonciade. The chapel stands in Place Georges Grammont, named after the benefactor whose gift of ten statues and around sixty canvases set the museum up in 1937. Today it is one of the finest galleries in France covering the work of artists active in the period 1890 to 1940. The gallery includes works by Bonnard, Matisse and Signac among others.

There are two other museums in the town: the **Musée Naval** in the Citadel, the sixteenth century fortress dominating the hill at the eastern edge of the town, has a collection of old engravings of the town, information on the Allied landings in 1944 and various other sea-based collections. The view from the Citadel alone is worth the journey, covering the Golfe de St Tropez and the Maures and Esterel hills. The **Maison des Papillons** (Museum of Butterflies) in Rue Etienne Berny is a fine Provençal house has a collection of 25,000 butterflies, including all native French species and thousands of exotic varieties.

St Torpes

St Tropez is named for St Torpes, a Roman centurion beheaded in 68AD, on Nero's orders, in Pisa for his faith. Legend has it that St Torpes' body and head were set adrift in a boat together with a dog and a cockerel who, it was anticipated, would eat the remains as a final humiliation. When the boat washed up here the remains were miraculously intact. The body was a treasured relic, but was lost in the eighth century when the Saracens attacked the town.

St Tropez is famous for its *bravades*, street processions of folk in character costume. At times other than *bravades*, the procession comprises The stars, the would-be stars and the curious. Ever since Brigitte Bardot exploded her bikini-based bomb on an unsuspecting world here in 1956, St Tropez has had a reputation for glitter. Bardot was advertising *And God Created Woman*, Roger Vadim's seminal film, but she stayed on, buying a villa in which she still lives devoting her time to animal welfare and opening a (now-closed) boutique.

Though many of the visitors are drawn by St Tropez's reputation, they are held by the undoubted charms of the port. Along Quai d'Épi on the western (car park) side of the old port's basin, artists show their paintings and work on their latest masterpieces aware, no doubt, that visitors exiting the nearby Annunciation Museum have had their appetite's for art whetted.

From the Quai, the view across the basin is superb, the expensive boats backed by the warm toned houses of Quai Suffren and Quai Jean Jaures with the Italianate bell tower of the town church peeping above them.

The Old Town with its exclusive boutiques lies close to the church, but for many the Quais are the essence of St Tropez. From them, in summer, boats will take you around the Gulf of St Tropez and even further afield. On Quai Suffren stands a statue of the Admiral de Suffren (1729-88) who, with only five ships under his command, harassed the English fleets from the West Indies to the Indian Ocean. The admiral (who had only been made a captain at the age of 55) died after blood-letting for a trivial problem. Château Suffren, the family home, is in the Old Town, near the town hall.

The St Tropez Bravades

St Torpes is commemorated in one of two venerable *bravades* (acts of defiance) that take place every year. The first takes place between 16 and 18 May, a gilded bust of St Torpes being carried round the town by a corps of a hundred *bravadeurs* dressed in eighteenth-century costume and making a thunderous noise with muskets, blank cartridges and music. Bystanders join in the fun and, on the last day, the procession makes its way to the pretty sixteenth-century Chapelle Ste-Anne, on a rock just south of the town.

The second *bravade* is on 15 June. This, the *Fête des Espagnols*, pays homage to the valiant Tropéziens for putting to flight the Spanish fleet in 1637 during the Thirty Years' War.

Shopping and Eating in St Tropez

The best of the shops in the town are concentrated in the streets close to the port: try **Rue Clemenceau** and **Rue Gambetta** which both run inland. The shops include well-known names as well as more local brands, and plenty of places where the famous *Tropézienne* sandals (based on an ancient design) can be bought. Chose the right shop and you can watch your pair being made.

For a coffee, any of the bars on Quai Suffren overlooking the port will do – choose the one where you can get a seat. For a meal try:

Le Mouscardins (FF)
Quai Jaurés,
near the Tour du Portalet
☎ 94 97 29 00
Provençal cooking, including the best bouillabaisse for many a mile.

Petit Charron (F)
6 Rue Charrons
(which runs away from the port,
on the Annociade side)
☎ 94 97 73 78
Very pleasant surroundings and a varied menu.

St Tropez is the only Riviera town which faces north, a fact which makes winters in the town much less appealing than summers. The setting, together with the lack of beaches on the Golfe shore, means that visitors wanting to see bikinis put to their as-manufactured use must head south to the **Anse de Pampelonne** which has a continuous line of private beaches. The sunbathing here is superb, but the swimming is less so, the collection of boats moored close to the shore, their owners and occupants brought ashore in dinghies, adding too much diesel fuel to the water for the comfort of the eyes of many bathers.

A Tour of the Maures from St Tropez

A fine drive from St Tropez explores the Massif des Maures to the west. From the roundabout outside the town, take the N98 to **Cogolin** where the workshops of the local carpet and fabric industry – set up in the early twentieth century by Armenian refugees – can be visited. Hand-weaving is still carried out here. Carpet making is only one of several local industries, along with cork making and the manufacture of musical instruments and furniture from local grown canes.

From Cogolin the N98 follows the Môle Valley, a mixture of forests and vines. much of the forest being cork oak and chestnut. At the Col de Gratteloup there is an arboretum, mainly devoted to Mediterranean tree species.

Bormes-les-Mimosas

Continue along the N98, then turn right along the D559, soon reaching a left turn for Bormes-les-Mimosas, an old, exquisitely sited, hill village. In that sense it is like many other Provençal villages, and would probably have remained a place for the connoisseur had it not been 'adopted' by artists and holiday home owners. Careful restoration of the houses, the planting of the mimosas of the name – together with oleander, bougainvillaea, camomile and eucalyptus – and the tending of window boxes and giant pots, have turned Bormes into a showpiece village. The addition to the name, reflecting the coming of age of the tourist and floral village, occurred in 1968. Within the village it is best to wander at leisure. Art and craft shops abound, but there are a few gems that should not be missed.

Place St François has a statue of St Francis de Paolo, who saved the village from plague in 1481, and a chapel dedicated to the saint. The village church, to St Trophyme, is eighteenth century and has a series of paintings – by Alain Nonn in 1980 – illustrating the path to the Cross. Of the old streets, be sure to find Rue Rompi-Cuou. The name of this very steep, shaded – and therefore damp – street is Provençal and reflects its slippery, hazardous nature. In polite company it is best to translate it as 'bottom breaker'.

Finally, the town museum is worth visiting. Its history collection explores the evolution of Bormes (and the Chartreuse de la Verne to the north), while its art collection reflects the work of local artists, particularly Jean-Charles Cazin.

Back to St Tropez

Beyond the Bormes the D559 reaches the coast at **Le Lavandou**, an underrated resort with a fine beach, a delightful central square, laid out as a garden, and views to the Iles d'Hyères. On again, the road passes through a string of small resorts, each with its individual character: St Clair, La Fossette, Aiguebelle, Cavalière. Ahead now is

Cork Making

Stripping the bark from the evergreen cork oak first takes place when the tree is about 25 years old and is then carried out every 10 years. Stripping always takes place in July or August when the tree's sap is rising so that there is time for a new layer of cork to be produced. Until the 1960s cork production in the Maures exceeded 5,000 tons annually, but has now dropped to less than 1,000 tons. In large part this decrease is due to the use of plastic corks by some wine producers. Plastic has some advantages, not least the cost, but is disliked by wine connoisseurs and, strangely, by conservationists. While it might be supposed that the bark stripping, which hardly enhances the looks of the trees, might be frowned upon by the Green lobby, the industry does preserve the cork oak forests: environmentalists fear that the loss of the cork industry will mean the destruction of the trees.

La Croix-Valmer. A right turn here follows the D93 around the Rama-teulle headland for a picturesque route back to St Tropez, crossing the Col de Collebasse.

Beyond the Col take a left turn to **Ramateulle**, a wonderful medieval village its houses arranged in tight circles within the line of the old defensive walls, then visit the **Moulin de Paillas**, three ruined windmills close to which is a viewpoint offering a magnificent panorama of the Esterel hills beyond the Golfe de St Tropez.

Bormes-les-Mimosas

Musée Arts et Histoire
65 Rue Carnot
Open: All year, July and August
Monday, Wednesday to Saturday
10am-12noon, 4-6pm Sunday
10am-12noon; also open Wednesday, Friday and Sunday 9-11pm;
September to June Wednesday
10am-12noon, 3-5pm, Sunday
10am-12noon. ☎ 94 71 56 60

Cogolin

Les Tapis et Tissues de Cogolin
(Carpets and Fabrics Workshop)
10 Boulevard Louis-Blanc
Open: All year, Monday to Friday
8.30am-12noon, 2-6pm.
☎ 94 54 66 17

Bormes-les-Mimosas

Frejus

L'Amphithéâtre (Roman Arena)
Open: All year, daily except
Tuesday 9am-12noon, 2-6.30pm
(4.30pm October to March).
☎ 94 51 34 31

Le Groupe Episcopal
(Cathedral Close)
Open: All year, April to September
daily 9-7pm; October to March daily
except Tuesday 9am-12noon,
2-5pm.
A single ticket covers the cathedral,
baptistery, cloister and museum.
Tickets are available from the
cloister. ☎ 94 51 26 30

La Pagode Bouddhique
Follow Avenue du XVe Corps
(the N7) for 1.2 miles (2km)
north of Fréjus
Open: All year, May to September
daily 9am-7pm; October to April
10am-6pm). ☎ 94 53 25 29

Memorial d'Indochine
Follow Avenue du XVe Corps
(the N7) for 1.2 miles (2km)
north of Fréjus
Open: All year, daily except
Tuesday 10am-5.50pm.
☎ 94 44 42 90

Musée des Troupes de Marine
(Marine Corps Museum)
3 miles (5km) north of the
town on the D4
Open: All year, June to September
daily except Tuesday 10am-12noon, 2-5.30pm; October to May
daily except Tuesday 2-5.30pm.
☎ 94 40 81 75

Parc Zoologique de Fréjus
3 miles (5km) west of
Fréjus on the N7
Open: All year, May to September
daily 9.30am-6pm; October to April
daily 10am-5pm. ☎ 94 40 70 65

Mandelieu-La Napoule

Château de la Napoule
Boulevard Henry Clews
Mandelieu-La Napoule
Open: March to October.
Guided tours daily at 3pm and 4pm

The red rocks of the Esterel coast make a perfect sunbathing terrace

(also 5pm in July and August).
☎ 93 49 95 05

St Raphaël

Musée Archéologique
Place de la Vieille Église
Open: All year, mid-June to mid-September daily except Tuesday 10am-12noon, 3-6pm; mid-September to mid-June daily except Sunday 10am-12noon, 2-5pm. ☎ 94 82 15 00

Church of St-Pierre-des-Templiers
Closed for restoration at the time of writing. Enquire at the Tourist Information Office, Rue Waldweck Rousseau ☎ 94 19 52 52.

St Tropez

L'Annonciade
Rue de la Nouvelle Poste
Open: All year (except November), June to September daily except Tuesday 10am-12noon, 3-7pm; October, December to May daily except Tuesday 10am-12noon, 2-6pm. ☎ 94 97 04 01

Maison des Papillons
(Museum of Butterflies)
Rue Etienne Berny

Open: All year, April to September daily except Tuesday 10am-12noon, 3-7pm; October to March daily except Sunday 3-6pm.
☎ 94 97 63 45

Musée de la Marine
Citadelle
Open: All year (except November), daily except Tuesday 10am-6pm (5pm in winter). ☎ 94 97 59 43

Ste Maxime

Musée des Traditions Locales
Tour Carrée des Dames
Place Aliziers
Open: All year, July to September daily except Tuesday 10am-12noon, 4-7pm; October to March daily except Tuesday 3-6pm; April to June daily except Tuesday 10am-12noon, 3-6.30pm.
☎ 94 96 70 30

Musée du Phonographer et de la Musique Mécanique
Parc de St Donat
5 miles (8km) north of
Ste Maxime, on the D25
Open: Easter to October Wednesday to Sunday 10am-12noon, 3-6pm. ☎ 94 96 50 42

For those heading east from Nice there is a choice of four roads: the A8 autoroute, and the three famous Corniche roads. The Grande Corniche (D2564), built by Napoleon, is the 19 mile (31km) high route between Nice and Menton. Use this road for the impressive views and for visiting the majestic Roman Trophy of the Alps at La Turbie. The Moyenne Corniche (N7) also provides excellent viewpoints: it is the direct route to Éze. The Corniche (N98) winds along the coast. Side roads connect all three Corniches.

GRANDE CORNICHE

On the Grande Corniche, after the viewpoints (that from the Hôtel Vistaëro is, by common consent, the best) comes **La Turbie**. The old section of the village is worth visiting for its picturesque houses and the church, built in the eighteenth century in Nice Baroque style. Inside it has some excellent art, mostly copies of work by famous artists, but still worth a look. The fountain at the end of the Avenue de la Victoire is fed by water from the old Roman aqueduct.

But it is another Roman ruin which draws the visitor – the vast remains of the Alpine Trophy, built on the Via Julia Augusta.

Alpine Trophy

The trophy commemorates the defeat of the Alpine tribes of Gaul by the Emperor Augustus and was erected in about 10BC. When complete – as shown in the site museum – the trophy stood 165ft (50m) tall, a conical top held aloft by a circle of columns standing on a square plinth. What remains – and the Trophy is one of only two that survive, the other being in Romania – is a section 115ft (35m) high including part of the columned circle.

The trophy can be climbed, the ascent giving a real feel for its engineering brilliance and majesty. One of the few sections of the original to remain complete (though this has been restored) is the inscription listing the titles of Augustus and noting his subjugation of, and listing, the 45 Alpine tribes. Some historians claim that this inscription is the first paragraph of the history of France.

Laghet

From La Turbie it is a short distance, going beneath the A8, to Laghet, where the sanctuary church of Notre-Dame de Laghet, an old pilgrimage church, still attracts votive offerings from Italy as well as France. A small museum in Place du Sanctuaire has a collection of the best of those offerings.

The Jardin Exotique at Èze

The Moyenne Corniche

The Moyenne Corniche crosses the Col de Villefranche, from where there is the best of the views, to reach **Èze**, a hill village perched on a rocky spire that offers excellent views towards the coast.

Near the car park, just off the main road, is a Fragonard perfumery. From the car park the visitor must walk steeply up to the village. The village is no less steep, any exploration involving climbing, but the effort is worthwhile, the old houses – many now art or craft shops – being very picturesque. The fourteenth century Chapelle des Pénitents has some excellent artwork.

The climbing eventually reaches the summit of the rock spire and the **Jardin Exotique**, a stunning array of cacti and succulents. The spire is topped by the ruins of a fourteenth century castle dismantled on the orders of Louis XIV. From the ruins, on clear mornings, Corsica can be seen.

Finally, visitors with time to spare can follow the Sentier Frédéric Nietzsche which descends from the village, through pines and olives, to Èze-Bord-de-Mer. It was on this old mule track that Nietzsche is said to have thought through the final section of *Thus Spoke Zarathustra*. The visitor should bear in mind that such thoughts are not guaranteed, and that the only way back to the village is along the same track – uphill all the way. If you do decide to try, allow two hours for the return journey.

Villefranche-sur-Mer

On the Lower Corniche, the visitor soon reaches Villefranche-sur-Mer whose excellent anchorage was acknowledged as soon as men started sailing the Mediterranean, though the name reflects its fourteenth century refounding as a 'free town'.

Making a Splash

In 1538 a peace conference in Nice, with the Pope as mediator, was seeking to reconcile King François I of France and Emperor Charles V of the Holy Roman Empire. The Emperor was staying in his ship moored at Villefranche and was visited by his sister (François' wife) and other local lords of high office. As the party made their way up the gangplank from the quay, the walkway collapsed, dumping the whole party into the sea. No one was hurt, but dignities were waterlogged and egos bruised. Though long ago, the incident still causes amusement in the town.

Villefranche's Old Town – north of the sixteenth-century Citadelle – is well worth exploring: take time to visit the Chapelle St-Pierre which was decorated in 1957 by Jean Cocteau. Cocteau sought to retell the life of the fisherman disciple, relating it to the lives of the town's fisherfolk.

Close to the Citadelle are two museums. In the first is a collection of work of the local sculptor Volti. The second building houses the

Goetz-Boumeester collection of work by those artists, husband and wife Henri Goetz and Christine Boumeester, who were active in the first half of this century, together with souvenir works by artists such as Picasso and Miró.

The Citadelle itself, built in the 1560s, houses a collection of archaeological items retrieved from a sixteenth century Genoese ship wrecked in the anchorage and the Roux collection of ceramic figures arranged in tableaux illustrating life in medieval times.

St Jean-Cap-Ferrat

It is necessary to leave the Corniche to drive around St Jean-Cap-Ferrat, but the detour is well worthwhile. Soon you will reach the **Villa Ephrussi de Rothschild**, the finest villa on the Riviera, in a setting that defies description.

The villa, a symbol of the *belle époque*, was built in the early 1900s to house the antique furniture and art collection of Baroness Ephrussi de Rothschild. In glorious Italian style, its pink walls, white windows, columns and balconies make it look even more fantastic and a splendid setting for the collections. The furniture, some of which belonged to Marie Antoinette, is set off by rich carpets and tapestries.

Outside, the 17 acres (7 hectares) of gardens are formally laid out with a large pond complete with fountain, and a double channel waterfall. With dragonflies darting over the ponds, the views of the house and the romantic setting beside the turquoise sea, it is difficult to imagine a more perfect site.

Cap-Ferrat from near Villefranche-sur-Mer

On the *cap* road, beyond the villa, there is a small **zoo** with around 300 species of birds and animals. The road now continues to the headland where the lighthouse can be climbed for a tremendous panorama, from Bordighera Point in Italy to the Esterel and the peaks of the Maritime Alps. Below the lighthouse a swimming pool has been hollowed from the rocks. One final interesting spot on the *cap* is Point St Hospice, the finger of land that pokes out eastwards from the main peninsula. The tip of this finger is rounded by a very pleasant walk, with fine views to Èze and Monaco.

Beaulieu

Back on the main Lower Corniche, Beaulieu is the next town reached. It is a fashionable, though far less hectic than those resorts to the west. Take a stroll through the gardens beside Boulevard Alsace-Lorraine or relax in the sheltered Baie des Fourmis.

On the bay's eastern tip is **Villa Kérylos**, a faithfully reproduced ancient Greek house built by Theodore Reinach, a Hellenistic scholar, during the 1900s. The frescoes and murals are copies, or variations, of originals and the materials – marble, alabaster, wood, leather etc – are, as far as possible, authentic. Some of the artwork is original and though most of the furniture is from the time of building, Greek ideas on design have been followed. The villa's name means 'sea swallow' in Greek.

Continuing eastward the visitor now passes below Èze to reach Monaco.

Beaulieu

Villa Kérylos
(Fondation Théodore Reinach)
Avenue Gustave Eiffel
Open: All year (except mid-November to mid-December), July and August daily 10am-7pm; September daily 10am-6pm; at other times Monday to Friday 10.30-6pm (2-6pm in December to February), Saturday and Sunday 10.30am-12.30am, 2-6pm.
☎ 93 01 01 44

Cap Ferrat

Cap Ferrat Lighthouse
Closed at the time of writing. Contact Tourist Office in St Jean-Cap-Ferrat.
(☎ 93 76 08 90) for details.

Parc Zoologique
Open: All year, March to September daily 10am-7pm (11pm in July and August); October to April Daily 9.30am-5pm. ☎ 93 76 07 60

Villa et Jardins Ephrussi de Rothschild
Open: All year, mid-February to October daily 10am-6pm (7pm in July and August); November to mid-February Monday to Friday 2-6pm Saturday and Sunday 10am-6pm.
☎ 93 01 33 09

Èze

Jardin Exotique
Open: All year, July and August daily 9am-8pm; September to June daily 9am-12noon, 2-5pm (7pm Easter to June). ☎ 93 41 10 30

La Turbie

Le Trophée des Alpes
Open: All year, April to September daily except Monday 9.30am-6pm; October to March daily except Monday 10am-5pm.
☎ 93 41 20 84

Places to Visit: Nice to Monaco

Laghet

Sanctuaire de Notre-Dame de Laghet
La Trinité
(Reached from La Turbie or the A8 exit at La Turbie)
Open: All year, daily 3-5pm.
☎ 93 41 09 60

Villefranche-sur-Mer

Chapelle St Pierre
(Chapelle Cocteau)
1 Quai Courbet, Port de la Santé
Open: All year (except mid-November to mid-December), July to September daily except Monday 9.30am-12noon, 2-6pm; October to mid-November daily except Monday 9.30am-12noon, 2-5pm; mid-December to March daily except Monday 9.30am-12noon, 3-7pm; April to June daily except Monday 9.30am-12noon, 4-8.30pm.
☎ 93 76 90 70

Fondation Volti
La Citadelle
Open: All year (except November), July and August Monday, Wednesday-Saturday 10am-12noon, 3-7pm, Sunday 3-7pm; September, October, December to June, Monday, Wednesday-Saturday 10am-12noon, 2-5pm, (3-6pm June to September), Sunday 2-5pm (3-6pm June to September). ☎ 93 76 33 27

Musée Goetz-Boumeester
La Citadelle
Open: All year (except November), July and August Monday, Wednesday-Saturday 10am-12noon, 3-7pm, Sunday 3-7pm; September, October, December to June, Monday, Wednesday-Saturday 10am-12noon, 2-5pm, (3-6pm June to September), Sunday 2-5pm (3-6pm June to September). ☎ 93 76 33 44

Musée Roux
La Citadelle
Open: All year (except November), July and August Monday, Wednesday-Saturday 10am-12noon, 3-7pm, Sunday 3-7pm; September, October, December to June, Monday, Wednesday-Saturday 10am-12noon, 2-5pm, (3-6pm June to September), Sunday 2-5pm (3-6pm June to September).
☎ 93 76 33 33

The Villa Ephrussi is one of the loveliest on the Riviera

6 Monaco

The Principality of Monaco, covering an area of under 500 acres (200 hectares) and with a population of only 25,000, is a sovereign state enclave surrounded by the *département* of Alpes-Maritimes. However, there are no frontier formalities even though the police uniform is different and distinctive.

The state consists of the capital town, Monaco, from whose Royal Palace it is administered, the resort of Monte-Carlo, and the commercial heart of La Condamine – not that much open space is available to separate one from another. So precious is land that in the last 30 years or so the Principality has transformed itself into tier upon tier of skyscrapers and reclaimed strips of land from the sea to create something by way of imported sand beaches.

Monaco's name derives from a temple to *Monoïkos* (Hercules) erected on the rock by Phoenicians. After the capture of the rock by the first Grimaldi ruler, Monaco was officially bought from the Genoese in 1308. It has been ruled by the Grimaldi family ever since, though there have been times of domination by the Spanish, the French and the Sardinians, and occasional disputes between various members of the Grimaldi family, several of them ending in assassinations.

Francesco the Spiteful and the Grimaldi Coat-of-Arms

In the late thirteenth century the rock on which the Palais du Prince now stands was in the hands of the city state of Genoa, the Genoese building a fortress on its summit. This was the time when the Holy Roman Empire was in internal conflict, with disputes between the pro-Papacy Guelfs and the pro-Emperor Ghibellines.

In 1297 Ghibelline Genoa expelled the Guelf Francesco (or François) Grimaldi. Grimaldi was known as Francesco the Spiteful and lived up to his name. He disguised himself as a monk and knocked on the door of the Monaco fortress. When the soldiers let him in he pulled a knife, killing several and holding the door open so his followers could gain access to kill the remainder. Today the Grimaldi coat-of-arms includes two armed monks as a tribute to the first Grimaldi ruler of the rock.

Nowadays Monaco, and particularly Monte-Carlo, is renowned as the playground of the rich. Behind such titles there is usually an ostentatiousness that amounts to vulgarity. Not so here, the whole of Monaco being quite genteel, its wealth distinctly underplayed. There is a thoughtfulness about the town planning – all new buildings must have underground parking to reduce the traffic problems, and there are lifts and escalators everywhere to help locals and visitors alike cope with the steepness of the site – and a satisfying lack of pretence. There is also an air of quiet confidence about the place: it comes as no surprise to discover that there is virtually no crime and that the streets are quite safe for pedestrians, even late at night. Many have attributed this to the reign of Prince Rainier, the present head of the Grimaldis, and especially to his late wife, the former American actress Grace Kelly who died tragically in 1982.

Although the wealth is understated it is still clearly present, as evidenced by the vast, shiny yachts in the Harbour and the year long schedule of events, some of them the highlight of the European social calendar – none more so than the Monaco Grand Prix, still the premier round of the Formula 1 world championship.

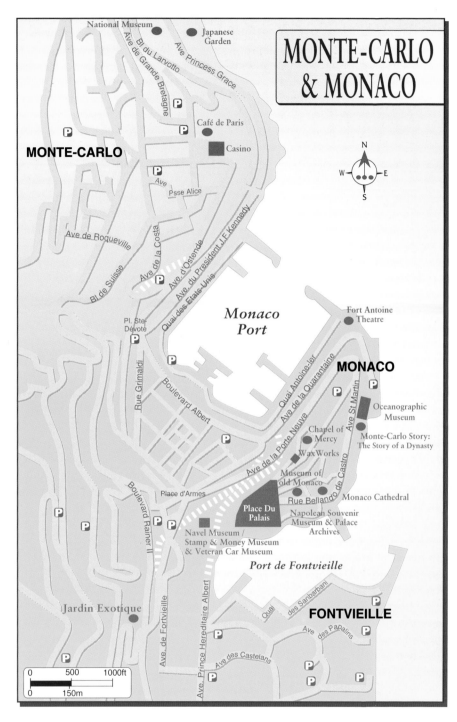

MONTE-CARLO & MONACO

MONTE-CARLO

National Museum

Japanese Garden

Café de Paris

Casino

Ave Psse Alice

Ave de Roqueville

Bl du Larvotto

Ave de Grande Bretagne

Ave Princess Grace

N
W E
S

Ave de la Costa

Ave d'Ostende

Ave du President J.F.Kennedy

Quai des Etats-Unis

Bl de Suisse

Monaco Port

Fort Antoine Theatre

Pl. Ste Dévote

Rue Grimaldi

Boulevard Albert

Quai Antoine-ler

Ave de la Quarantaine

MONACO

Ave St Martin

Oceanographic Museum

Chapel of Mercy

Monte-Carlo Story: The Story of a Dynasty

Ave de la Porte Neuve

WaxWorks

Museum of old Monaco

Place d'Armes

Boulevard Rainer II

Rue Bellando de Castro

Monaco Cathedral

Place Du Palais

Napolean Souvenir Museum & Palace Archives

Navel Museum / Stamp & Money Museum & Veteran Car Museum

Port de Fontvieille

Jardin Exotique

Ave de Fortvieille

Ave Prince Hereditaire Albert

Quai des Sanbarbani

FONTVIEILLE

Ave des Papalins

Ave des Castelans

0   500   1000ft
0   150m

The first Grand Prix around the streets of Monaco was held in 1929, races continuing until the outbreak of World War II. In 1950 when the first official championship series was held, the very first race was at Silverstone in Britain and the Monaco Grand Prix was the year's second race. A ten-car crash on the first lap eliminated a good proportion of the field, the race being won by Juan Manuel Fangio who many still regard as the greatest driver of all time.

Monaco did not hold a Grand Prix in 1951, 1953 or 1954, and the 1952 race was for sports cars only. But then in 1955 the Grand Prix was held again and it has been held every year since. In the 1960s British driver Graham Hill was the 'King of Monaco' winning five times. Then in a remarkable 10 year period from 1984 to 1993 Alain Prost (4 victories) and Ayrton Senna (6 victories) won every race.

The track has changed over the years, a new chicane being added near the tunnel exit and the swimming pool (to try and reduce the speed of the cars) adding a new hazard by the Harbour. The lack of opportunities for overtaking have led some to question the suitability of the circuit for modern cars, but the skill of the drivers in negotiating the tight turns of the hairpin and managing to avoid the barriers still makes for a wonderful spectacle. Moreover, how could anyone even contemplate consigning names like Casino Square, Ste Devote, Rascasse and Mirabeau to history's dustbin?

The famous hairpin on the Grand Prix circuit

MONTE-CARLO

Our tour of Monaco starts at the **Casino** in Monte-Carlo, arguably the most famous site in the Principality. The building dates from 1878 when it was rebuilt by Charles Garnier, architect of the Paris Opera House, but has additions from later times. It is a sumptuous place and beautifully set with a garden terrace at the rear – from which, at the southern end, there are tremendous views of the Harbour and the Monaco rock – and the picturesque Place de Casino and the rectangle of the Allée de Boulingrins beyond. The Allée is used as an open air art gallery with

• THE MONTE-CARLO CASINO •

In the 1850s the Principality was facing bankruptcy and the Prince, Charles III, sought ways of raising finance. He sold Roquebrune and Menton to the French and then allowed the building of a casino. The venture was only partially successful and there were no great hopes when the gaming moved to a new, purpose-built site on a hill to the east of the Harbour. But the arrival of a new director, François Blanc changed both the casino and the Principality for ever. Soon the building was providing enough cash for the Prince's purse for taxes to be abandoned – the grateful citizens named the hill below the casino Monte Carlo in tribute to the Prince: Monagesques still pay no taxes, though VAT is chargeable on all goods sold. At one time gambling contributed 95 per cent of the Principality's income. Today the figure is around 5 per cent, Monaco having become highly efficient (and tax efficient) in business and commerce.

There are many stories about the casino, most of them exaggerated and others probably untrue. A British Prime Minister was thrown out for not having his passport, a man put all his money on the numbers of the hymns set up in his local church for morning service – and won. The man who broke the bank, the inspiration for the famous song, was Charles Deville Wells, a British swindler did indeed break it several times, but his winnings never came to more than £10,000 in a single win (though that is hardly to be sneezed at, especially at 1890 values) but the Casino eventually got its money back and more besides, successfully breaking Wells who returned home penniless and was arrested and imprisoned for the crimes that had bankrolled his spree.

Then as now the house is usually the winner. Before being tempted to don your white tie and look out your passport it is worth remembering what used to be said in François Blanc's time. On the roulette wheel the win was sometimes rouge, sometimes noir. But it was always Blanc.

regularly changing sculptures.

Many visitors are so enthralled by the casino square that they want to stop for a drink at the pavement cafés on the northern side, which include the famous Café de Paris, but the prices at these are steep. If you consider it worthwhile for the view and the experience, fine, but otherwise use the cafés in nearby Avenue des Spelugues. At the latter not only are prices cheaper, but are on the route of the Grand Prix.

North of the Casino, beyond the famous hairpin, is the **National Museum**, housed in a delightful villa built by Garnier, the architect of the Casino. The museum houses the Galea collection of dolls and automatons, one of the best of its kind in Europe and a must for enthusiasts. There are also annual exhibitions in keeping with the collection – teddy bears for example.

North again, but close to the museum, is Plages du Larvotto, the best of the Principality's public beaches. Also close to the museum – a little closer to the Casino and down by the sea – is the **Jardin Japonais** with ponds of koi carp, delightful Japanese-style bridges and a tea room.

MONACO

From the Casino, wide pavements and steps take the visitor over the tunnel used by the Grand Prix to the quayside. To the right as you walk along is La Condamine, packed with shops catering for everyone from the casual visitor to the seriously rich. Ahead, after a pleasant quay-side walk past the swimming pool a steep path leads up the side of Monaco's Rock to the Place du Palais.

The Palace itself (the **Palais du Prince**) can be visited and is worthwhile for its elegant decoration and for the **Musée Napoléonien**. The Princes of Monaco are distant relatives of the old Emperor and have amassed an interesting collection of memorabilia. The museum also houses the **Archives du Palais**, an archive collection on the history of the Principality, with stamps, coins and medals as well as documents.

From the Palace there are fine views of Fontvieille and its port, and the changing of the guard outside, daily at 11.55am precisely, is worth waiting for.

On the other side of the Place du Palais there is a fine viewpoint of the Harbour and Monte Carlo. Nearby is the **Historial des Princes de Monaco** where scenes from the Principality's past are enacted in twenty or so dioramas with forty full-size wax models.

Also on the rock is the **cathedral**, built in the late nineteenth century in neo-Romanesque style. The cathedral has some fine early paintings and a splendid altar piece by Louis Bréa.

Heading towards the point of the rock Place de la Visitation is reached. Here the seventeenth century Baroque chapel houses an important collection of sacred art including works by Rubens and some Italian masters (the **Musée de la Chapelle de la Visitation**).

Musée Océanographique

Lastly on the rock is the Musée Océanographique, one of the foremost of its kind in the world. The museum was founded by Prince Albert I in 1910. In its basement is an aquarium of over 4,500 Mediterranean fish (some 400 species in all, swimming in 90 tanks), probably the best in Europe and certainly the most complete collection of Mediterranean species.

The ground floor has a collection illustrating the development of underwater exploration (much of it developed by Jacques Cousteau) and skeletons of sea creatures, including narwhal, sperm whale, orca and turtle, and a cast of a coelacanth. There is also a fine collection of shells. A small cinema shows films made by Cousteau.

The first floor illustrates Prince Albert's own voyages, marine phenomena (waves, tides etc). There is also a model of the Marianna Trench, the world's deepest oceanic trench, and an animated model of the sinking of the *Titanic*. From the Museum's terrace, or from nearby, the view is extensive, south-west towards Nice, Cap d'Antibes and the Esterel peaks, north-east to the Italian Riviera. Close to the headland the **Musée du Cinéma** has frequent audio-visual exploring the story of Monaco and Monte-Carlo.

FONTVIEILLE

On the western side of the Palace, but not accessible from the Place du Palais, is the **Jardin Animalier** (Monaco Zoo), with collections of mammals, birds and reptiles. From the Jardin there is a good view of the Fontvieille Harbour.

In this suburb are three museums and a fine park. The **Musée Naval** has around 150 model ships from all ages, including the battleships *Potemkin* and *Missouri*, and Napoleon's Imperial Gondola.

The **Collection des Voitures Anciennes** is Prince Rainier's car

As might be expected, all the major fashion, leather and jewelry houses have outlets, mostly in Monte-Carlo. Chanel is in Place du Casino, Yves St-Laurent Rive Gauche in Avenue des Beaux Arts and Gucci in Avenue de Monte-Carlo. The Niçois fashion house Chacok is in Avenue Princess Grace. Georges-Rech, another major fashion house has its outlet in Condamine, at 15 Rue de Millo. Adonis, at 39 Avenue Princess Grace, is an outlet for Jean-Paul Gaultier, Calvin Klein, Christian Lacroix, Gianni Versace and others. Slightly cheaper are Max Mara, which has an outlet in the Centre Commercial Le Métropole and Escada/Escada Sport are in Avenue de la Costa.

• SHOPPING IN MONACO •

The main leather outlets are in Monte-Carlo: **Louis Vuitton** in Avenue des Beaux Arts and **Hermès** in Avenue de Monte-Carlo. For jewelry the major outlets are **Bulgari** in Avenue des Beaux Arts, **Cartier** and **Van Cleef & Arpels** in Place du Casino.

Other major (which usually means expensive) shops are also to be found in Avenue des Beaux Arts and Place du Casino.

There are three commercial complexes, about the closest Monaco comes to a departmental store. The **Le Métropole Centre** in Monte-Carlo, a little way north of the Casino, is excellent for perfume, fashion and CDs/videos. The **Les Allées Lumières Centre** lies close to the far end of the Allée des Boulingrins from the Casino, while there is another complex in Fontvieille.

For the best in souvenirs, explore the narrow shops opposite the Monaco rock. As might be expected, Monaco has a great number of antique and art shops. It is best to explore the outlets – most of them in Monte-Carlo – but if you are pressed for time, try **Galerie Adriana Ribolzi Antiquaire** which has shops in Avenue Henry Dunant and Avenue l'Hermitage, and the **Galerie d'Art Ancien** et Moderne in Boulevard Princesse Charlotte.

Left & right: Monte Carlo is the place for exclusive shopping

Place des Armes, Monaco

collection, the second museum, includes a De Dion Bouton from 1903 and other very early European and American cars. A London taxi converted for use by Princess Grace and a helmet used by Ayrton Senna (in a section dealing with Grand Prix) are two poignant exhibits.

The third museum is the **Musée des Timbres et des Monnaie,** the Stamp and Coin Museum with collections covering Monaco's history. It includes many rare and historically important items.

The museums are all in Fontvieille's commercial heart which also has shops and cafés. Another example of considered planning is seen in Fontvieille: the Monegasques have even insisted on McDonalds toning down its usual garish signs so as to more readily reflect the required ambience.

Seawards from the middle of Fontvieille is **Espace Fontvieille**, a park which includes Princess Grace's Rose Garden with almost 4,000 varieties and a statue of the Princess executed by Kees Verkade in 1983. A reminder of the Principality's wealth is the park's heliport.

Another garden, but one quite different to the Princess' roses, lies above Fontvieille. The views alone from the **Jardin Exotique** make a visit worthwhile, but there is also a collection of over 6,000 cacti and succulents from all the world's desert and semi-deserts. Within the garden is the Observatory Cave, an interesting show cave with good formations. The cave was inhabited some 200,000 years ago, the excavated finds, and others from the Riviera region, being displayed in the Garden's **Musée d'Anthropologie Préhistorique.**

RESTAURANTS IN MONACO

It is easy to eat your way through a great deal of money in Monaco. At the very top of the range is the **Hôtel de Paris** in Place du Casino, Monte-Carlo has two restaurants which are at the very highest pinnacle in terms of standards, cuisine and price. They are:

Louis XV
☎ 92 16 30 01

Grill de l'Hôtel de Paris
☎ 92 16 29 66

Other places worth considering are:

Café de Paris (FF)
Place du Casino
Monte-Carlo, ☎ 92 16 20 20
Beautifully sited and decorated in early twentieth century style.

Le St Benoit (FF)
10 Avenue de la Costa
Monte-Carlo, ☎ 93 25 02 34
Superb seafood restaurant with a panoramic view.

Contact (F)
9 Avenue des Spelugues
Monte-Carlo, ☎ 93 15 97 97
Close to the Place du Casino. Much cheaper than the Café de Paris, especially if you are only looking for a coffee. Excellent menu and good service.

Pizzeria Monegasque (F)
Rue Terrazzini
Monaco, ☎ 93 30 16 38
Pizzas and charcoal grilled food in a pedestrianised street at the base of the rock.

**Below; Left: Fontvieille from Place du Palais
Right: Monaco from the Jardin Exotique**

Collection des Voitures Anciennes (Prince Rainier's Vintage Car Collection)
Les Terrasses de Fontvielle
Open: All year (except November), daily 10am-6pm. ☎ 92 05 28 56

Espace Fontvieille (including Princess Grace's Rose Garden)
Avenue des Papalins
Fontvieille
Open: All year, April to September daily 9am-7pm (8pm in July and August); October to March daily 9am-5pm. ☎ 92 16 61 16 for info

Historial des Princes de Monaco/Musée de Cires
(Waxworks)
27 Rue Basse, Monaco
Open: All year, daily 10am-6pm.
☎ 93 30 39 05

Jardin Animalier
Boulevard Charles III
Monaco
Open: All year, June to September daily 9am-12noon, 2-7pm; October to May daily 10am-12noon, 2-5pm (6pm from March to May).
☎ 93 25 18 31

Jardin Exotique
Musée d'Anthropologie Préhistorique and
Grotte de l'Observatoire
56bis Boulevard du Jardin Exotique
Monaco
Open: All year, May to September 9am-7pm; October to April 9am-6pm. ☎ 93 15 80 06

Musée de la Chapelle de la Visitation
Place de la Visitation
Monaco
Open: All year, daily except Monday 10am-4pm. ☎ 93 50 07 00

Musée du Cinéma
(Monte-Carlo Story)
Terrasses du Parking des Pêcheurs
Monaco
Open: All year, July and August daily 11am-6pm; March to June, September and October daily 11am-5pm; November-February daily 2-5pm. ☎ 93 25 32 33

Musée National de Monaco
17 Avenue Princesse Grace
Monte-Carlo
Open: All year, Easter to September daily 10am-6.30pm; October to Easter daily 10am-12.15pm, 2.30-6.30pm. ☎ 93 30 91 26

Musée Naval de Monaco
Les Terrasses de Fontvieille
Open: All year, daily 10am-6pm.
☎ 92 05 28 48

Musée Océanographique
Avenue St Martin
Monaco
Open: All year, April to September daily 9am-7pm; October to March daily 10am-6pm. Closed on the day of the Grand Prix. ☎ 93 15 36 00

Guards outside Monaco's Palace of the Princes

Musée du Souvenir Napoléonien et Archives du Palais Princier
Place du Palais
Monaco
Open: All year (except mid-November-mid-December), June to September daily 9.30am-6.30pm; October to mid-November daily 10am-5pm; December to May daily except Monday 10.30am-12.30pm, 2-5pm. ☎ 93 25 18 31

Musée des Timbres et des Monnaie
Les Terrasses de Fontvieille
Open: All year, daily 10am-5pm (6pm from June-September).
☎ 93 15 41 50

Palais Princier
Place du Palais
Monaco
Open: June to September daily 9.30am-6.30pm; October daily 10am-5pm. Guided tours (in English) available. ☎ 93 25 18 31

Right: The square in front of Monte Carlo's Casino

Below: The Palace of the Princes, Monaco

Menton & the Mercantour

7

MONACO TO MENTON

Northern of Monaco the corniche roads converge at Roquebrune-Cap-Martin. The new town lies beside the sea, but it is worth a short detour to visit the skillfully restored hill-village (usually called just Roquebrune in an effort to limit confusion).

Medieval houses and steep, arched-over alleys lead up to the *donjon* (keep), all that remains of the town's tenth-century castle, claimed to be the oldest in France. It is a fine sight when floodlit at night and deserves to be visited for the furnished apartments and primitive kitchen on the third floor. Above is a terrace from which Cap Martin can be seen, 985ft (300m) below.

On the afternoon of August 5, the visitor to Roquebrune can witness scenes from the Passion enacted between the village and the chapel of La Pausa. It is a 500-year-old tradition, fulfilling a vow made in 1467 by villagers who survived the plague.

A second traditional procession takes place on the evening of Good Friday when some villagers dress as Roman soldiers, with others dressed as disciples carrying a statue of Christ. The windows of Roquebrune are decorated with flowers and up-turned empty snail shells holding lighted wicks. The procession is known in Provençal as *Proucessioun dei Limassa*, (the Procession of the Snails). Its religious name is Procession of the Entombment of Christ. Some say the ritual dates back to 1316, the snails being a Christian symbol of resurrection.

Finally, about 220yd (200m) beyond the village limits, there is a famous olive tree thought to be 1,000 years old.

From the Lower Corniche a road reaches Cap Martin, from where there are wonderful views of the coast, then continues through olive groves to reach the new town of Roquebrune. Beside the road is **Le Corbusier's Bungalow** (Cabanon de Le Corbusier), designed as a model for minimal, modular living. Much of the furniture has several functions so as to accentuate the use of space. Le Corbusier did actually live in the bungalow: he is buried in the village cemetery in a tomb he designed himself.

MENTON

Now continue along the coast road for the brief journey to Menton. Although many modern buildings have been built outside the **Old Town**, Menton remains a picture-postcard Italianate town. Tall, honey-toned

The beach at Menton

A Menton legend states that when God expelled Adam and Eve from the Garden of Eden, Eve took a lemon with her. When the pair found the site on which Menton now stands, Eve decided it was an earthly paradise and planted the seeds from her lemon. All local lemon trees are said to stem from those seeds.

For centuries Menton's prosperity was based on lemons: it is said that when Roquebrune and Menton were sold by Monaco to France it was due not only to the Monaco Prince's poverty but to agitation from local lemon growers who knew that France was a better market than Italy for their crop. It is also said that when the British ambassador heard the price France was paying he shook his head and said it was an awful lot of money for a few lemons.

Today, the lemon's part in the town's history is celebrated at the annual lemon festival in February. The festival is focused around the Biovès Gardens (at the western end of the seafront) where 100 tons or more of citrus fruits are used to create giant tableaux. The festival includes a procession of fruit decorated floats on three consecutive Sundays.

Tons of fruit are used to create impressive works of art during Menton's Lemon Festival

houses rise gracefully from near the sea to the church of St Michel. Outside the church, a prestigious chamber-music festival is held under floodlights during the first half of August.

Menton's setting is idyllic. The mountains stand well back, respectfully, yet give the town its enviable winter climate which allows lemon crops to ripen. Queen Victoria's early visits to the Riviera were to Menton – the grateful town raised a statue to her – and she was followed by other members of the European aristocracy, and then by the great names of literature. Despite the stardom, compared with other resorts along the coast, Menton retains a more leisurely atmosphere.

Walking Tour of Menton

Start your exploration on the Promenade du Soleil, the sea front road which leads to Quai Napoleon III. In a bastion, built into the Harbour wall, is the **Cocteau Museum**, an important collection of work by an artist resident in Menton from 1957. From the Quai the view of the town falling down the hill towards the sea is breathtaking, particularly in the early morning before heat haze has blotted out the hills that tower above it. Quai Napoleon ends at a lighthouse, the other retaining arm finishing at Volti's statue of St Michael.

Follow the sea front past that quay (Jetée Impératrice-Eugénie) to reach, to the left, a surprising set of steps which lead to Parvis St-Michel, a distinctly Italian square overlooked by the town church. St Mi-chel's is claimed by many to be the finest Baroque church on the eastern Riviera. Inside there are some superb works: look out especially for the sixteenth century altarpiece.

The Old Town lies to the north of the church (turn right from the square). Especially good are Rue Longue – which intersects the steps at about half-height – and Rue Vieux-Château which leads to the old cemetery. The headstones are interesting for their well-known English names, Menton having first been used as a health resort for the treatment of tuberculosis on the initiative of the English specialist, Dr Henry Bennet, in the 1860s.

From the church, descend the steps on its right side and follow Rue St Michel through the shopping heart of the town. To the right after about 550yd (500m) a short walk leads to the **Town Hall** and **Cocteau's Marriage Hall**. All marriage ceremonies in France must have a civil component to be legal and all those in Menton are performed here.

The hall was entirely decorated by Cocteau – heavy black doors, Spanish seats and a series of allegorical paintings. Behind the stage a local boy and girl exchange loving glances. He has a fish for an eye, an old legend claiming that the truth of anyone's life is in their eyes – and he is a fisherman. The hall's main reception (used only for ceremonies) has mirrors set on a curve to give an illusion of infinity.

Marianne, French heroine

Those visiting Cocteau's Marriage Hall will see Marianne, the mythical French heroine whose image adorns the coinage and whose image must, by law, be in all town halls. Marianne was the heroine of the Revolution, adopted in 1789 to portray Liberty, the bare-breasted (and well-endowed) woman leading the charge of the men of France.

During World War II the Vichy regime banned portraits of Marianne, fearing her ability to rouse patriotism in the people. After 1945 portraits were again seen, although it was not until 1969 when Brigitte Bardot was appointed as the official model for Marianne (who is seen on banknotes and coins as well as in town halls) did she again capture the nation's imagination.

Recently there has been a competition for a new model to replace Catherine Deneuve who has been Marianne since 1985. The winner of a vote of French mayors was Laetitia Casta, a supermodel and actress.

Gardens near Menton

Leaving Menton on the road towards the Italian border, just a few miles away, the visitor soon reaches **Garavan** where the gardens of several luxurious villas built by rich residents are open to visitors. **Jardin du Val Rahmeh** is probably the most famous, a garden with over 700 species of trees, shrubs and flowers, many of them Mediterranean species, laid out by the British in the 1930s. **Jardin des Romanciers** surrounds the Villa Fontana Rosa, built by the Spanish novelist Blasco Ibañez. The villa stands in a pottery garden, with tiled pools and pergolas. **Jardin de Maria Serena** is claimed to have the most temperate climate in France, the temperature never having fallen below 40°F (5°C): it has a fine collection of palm trees. Finally, **Jardin des Colombières** is typically French, with a mix of formal features and architectural features, and more natural landscapes.

Continuing along the main street the visitor reaches **Jardin Biovès**, beautiful gardens surrounded by palm and lemon trees. The statues are by Volti. To the north of Biovès is the Palais Carnoles, an Italian style eighteenth century mansion that was formerly the summer palace of the Monacan Princes. It now houses the town's fine arts museum (**Musée des Beaux-Arts**) with contemporary work on the ground floor and work from the sixteenth to eighteenth centuries on the first floor.

Elsewhere in the town the **Palais de l'Europe**, in Avenue Boyer, houses a continuous cycle of exhibitions of contemporary art, while the **Musée de Préhistoire Réginales**, housed in a building, north of the Town Hall, designed specifically by the architect Adrien Rey, has collections from local sites, including the skull of Menton Man who lived here several hundred thousand years before the great boom in the town's prosperity.

THE ROYA VALLEY AND MERCANTOUR NATIONAL PARK

North of Menton the visitor can explore the Upper Roya Valley and the eastern section of the Mercantour National Park. The quickest approach is to cross into Italy, heading north from the A8's 'Ventimiglia' turn off.

This road, the S20, soon crosses the border again, reaching **Breil-sur-Roya**, a pleasant village, its old section still dotted with the remnants of gateways and defensive walls. Breil can also be reached by a route that stays in France, heading north on the D2566 from Menton to **Sospel** another excellent village, its 'eleventh century' bridge a copy of the original which was destroyed in World War II.

Close to the village, on Col St-Jean along the road to Nice, **Fort Suchet** (also called Le Barbonnet) houses the **Museum of the Alpine Army**, a tribute to men who survived cold and natural dangers as well as the more obvious threats of warfare, while **Fort St Roch** has a museum to resistance fighters.

North of Breil the Roya valley tightens at the **Saorge** Gorge, the village of the name hanging above the river in an almost surreal way. The village's steep, sometimes stepped and arched streets meander about the hillside in enchanting fashion: from the southern end the fine Romanesque church of Madonna del Poggio can be reached by a short walk, worthwhile for the fine Italian-style campanile and the excellent fifteenth century artwork.

North again the valley is increasingly tight and picturesque. At **St Dalmas-de-Tende**, a right turn should be made, going through **La Brigue** to visit the extraordinary chapel of **Notre-Dame des Fontaines**. In the fourteenth century seven springs (*fontaines*) watered the valley at this point but an earthquake sealed them off. The valley dwellers prayed to the Virgin for salvation and the springs miraculously began to flow again. In thanks they built a chapel which soon became an important pilgrimage site.

Back in the main valley, as you drive towards Tende it is worth reflecting that the Roya Valley has only been French since 1947. At the time of the transfer of Nice and its hinterland to France in 1860, the logical border – following the ridge of the Maritime Alps – was ignored

because the Italian king wished to preserve his beloved hunting ground!

Tende

Tende is the capital of the upper valley, an Italianate village of interesting narrow streets. The fifteenth century town church is the best example of the Italian Gothic style in the Maritime Alps.

From Tende the **Mercantour National Park** is easily explored. The Park was created in 1979, adjoining Italy's Argentera National Park, to protect the vegetation – which includes both alpine and Mediterranean species, and wildlife.

Half of France's wild flower species grow here, over forty of which bloom nowhere else in the country. The wildlife includes several rare species of butterfly, as well as marmot, ibex and chamois. The birdlife includes golden eagles and Tengmalm's Owl. The chief interest, however, lies in the rock engravings of the Vallée des Merveilles (the Valley of Marvels) surrounding Mont Bégo.

Notre-Dame des Fontaines

As befitted its status as a pilgrimage focal point, the chapel walls were frescoed. The chancel painted by the local Gothic master Jean Baleison and the nave by a genius of the primitive Renaissance school, Giovanni Canavesio. Baleison's works have not been well-served by time, but Canavesio's panels, telling the story of Jesus' life, are almost perfect, displaying an exuberance and enthusiasm that is stunning.

There is no compromise in the scenes, that of the hanging Judas being quite gruesome, the Crucifixion being unflinchingly painful and the Last Judgement, on the end wall, remorseless. It seems almost that Canavesio wanted to instruct the viewer – do not stray from the Christian path or this will be your fate. The effect of the panels on the superstitious medieval valley folk can well be imagined: after the service, they were confronted with the Last Judgement as they left, just to press the message home.

Above: St Michel in Menton is one of the Riviera's finest Baroque churches

Below: Today the water front at Menton is filled with pleasure, rather than fishing, boats

The Carvings of the Valley of Marvels

On rocks surrounding the peak some 100,000 engravings have been found, each produced from dots made by striking a sharp point (an antler for instance) against the rock. The engravings are of limited patterns – oxen pulling a plough, fields and houses represented as squares, daggers – but there are a small number of strange shapes. Of these a Christ-like head and a curious figure with feet turned in – the so-called Chief of the Tribe – are the most interesting.

Specialists fancy a Bronze Age date for the engravings, suggesting a religious significance. Mont Bégo is set where cold dry alpine air meets warm, moist Mediterranean air, and so sees many thunderstorms. It is also a ferritic mountain and so is frequently struck by lightning. It is thought that the early dwellers of the Mercantour noticed this and believed that gods lived in the peak, talking to the gods of the sky by means of lightning. They therefore completed their engravings (offerings to the gods) while looking at the peak: all the engravings are on rocks worn smooth by glaciers and face away from Mont Bégo.

To see the engravings, particularly the most interesting ones, it is essential to have a guide: the Merveilles is huge and there are countless rocks. It is also necessary to be prepared for a long hard day – the walk up to the valley takes several hours, although jeep transport can be arranged in Tende and St Dalmas. There are a few engravings in the Fontanable Valley which can be reached by car, but they are not easy to find. An alternative is the **Musée des Merveilles** in Tende. For information on guides, jeeps and the museum's opening times, ask at Tende's Information Centre.

North of Tende the main road uses a tunnel to cross into Italy, though the adventurous can use a multi-hairpin road to reach the **Col de Tende**, a fine viewpoint. From it, a short walk visits **Fort Central**, one of a line of forts built in about 1882 at a time of tension between France and Italy. The fort cannot be visited, except by the intrepid visitor, but is still a worthwhile destination. Those that do venture inside will be astonished at the size of the gun emplacements. The field of view meant that any army advancing up the Roya Valley would have found taking the Col very difficult.

From the Col with its view of high mountains, it is a drive of little more than an hour to Menton or Nice, where the visitor can watch the sun go down into the azure sea.

* = Closed on official holidays

Menton

Cocteau's
'Salles des Mariages' *
Mairie (Town Hall), Place Ardoïno
Rue de la République
Open: All year, Monday to Friday
8.30am-12.30pm, 1.30-5pm.
☎ 92 10 50 00

Jardin des Colombières
Route des Colombières
Closed for restoration at time of
writing. For details ☎ 92 10 33 66

Jardin de Maria Serena
21 Promenade Reine-Astrid
Open: All year
Guided tours only Tuesday at
10am. ☎ 92 10 33 66

Jardin des Romanciers
Villa Fontana Rosa
Avenue Blasco-Ibañez
Open: All year. Guided tours only
on second and fourth Friday and
third Saturday in each month at
10am. ☎ 92 10 33 66

Jardin du Val Rahmeh
Avenue St Jacques
Open: All year, May to September
daily 10am-12.30pm, 3-6pm;
October to April daily 10am-
12.30pm, 3-5pm. ☎ 93 35 86 72

Musée Cocteau *
Bastion du Vieux Port
2 Quai Napoléon III
Open: All year, daily except
Tuesday 10am-12noon, 2-6pm.
☎ 93 57 72 30

Musée du Palais Carnolès *
3 avenue de la Madone
Open: All year, June to September
daily except Tuesday 10am-
12noon, 3-7pm; October to May
daily except Tuesday 10am-
12noon, 2-6pm. ☎ 93 35 49 71

Musée de
Préhistoire Régionale *
Avenue Lorédan Larchey
Open: All year, June to September
daily except Tuesday 10am-
12noon, 3-7pm; October to May
daily except Tuesday 10am-
12noon, 2-6pm. ☎ 93 35 49 71

Palais de l'Europe *
(Museum of Contemporary Art)
Avenue Boyer
Open: All year, June to September
daily except Tuesday 10am-
12noon, 3-7pm; October to May
daily except Tuesday 10am-
12noon, 2-6pm. ☎ 93 35 49 71

Notre-Dame des Fontaines
Nr La Brigue
Open: All year, May to October
daily 9.30am-7pm; November to
April. Obtain key from cafés or
restaurants in La Brigue. They will
require a passport as security.
☎ 93 04 76 73 (La Brigue Town
Hall, for details)

Roquebrune-Cap-Martin

Château Musée
Place William Ingram,
Roquebrune Village
Open: All year (except November),
May to September daily except
Friday 10am-12noon, 2-7pm;
October, December to April daily
except Friday 10am-12noon,
2-6pm. Open on Fridays in school
holidays. ☎ 93 35 07 22

Le Corbusier's Bungalow
Promenade Le Corbusier
Open: All year, by appointment
only at 9.30am on Tuesdays.
☎ 93 35 62 87 to add your name
to the invitation list.

Sospel

Musée Armée des Alpes
Fort Suchet (Le Barbonnet)
Col St Jean
(On the D2204 Nice road)
Open: May to September, July and
August daily except Tuesday and
Friday. Guided tour at 3.30pm; all
other times Saturday and Sunday
guided tour at 3.30pm.
☎ 93 04 15 80

Musée de la Resistance
Fort St Roch
(Close to the village on the
D2204 Nice road)
Open: June to mid-September
daily except Monday 2-6pm; mid-
September to October Saturday
and Sunday 2-6pm.
☎ 93 04 00 09

Tende

Musée des Merveilles
Avenue 16 Septembre 1947
Open: All year, May to mid-October
daily except Tuesday 10.30am-
6.30pm (9pm on Saturday); mid-
October to April daily except
Tuesday 10.30am-5pm.
☎ 93 04 32 50

Menton

GETTING THERE

BY AIR

The Côte d'Azur is served by the international airport of **Nice-Côte d'Azur**, situated above the Mediterranean at the south-western end of the town. It is well connected to the autoroute system.

The airport is served by international flights and also has regular services to Paris.

There is also smaller airport served by more infrequent flights at Fréjus-St Raphaël.

There is a helicopter link between Nice-Côte d'Azur airport and Monaco.

BY RAIL

SNCF (Systéme National de Chemin-de-Fer), the French national railway company, has both fast and express trains linking the Côte d'Azur with other parts of France and the Channel ports. Of particular interest to the visitor keen to cut down on travel time is the **TGV** (pronounced Tay-Jay-Vay) service, a very fast 155mph (250kph) bullet-shaped train that speeds between Paris and the south. The TGV offers only first class accommodation but does cut journey time considerably.

SNCF also offer motorail services to those not wishing to spend a part of their holiday gazing at the ribbon of the Autoroute du Soleil. These services are available from the Channel ports, but not to Fréjus-St Raphaël or Nice – for those services the visitor must first reach Paris. The service is not cheap but the journey is overnight, which does have the advantage of extending the holiday by a day if travelling is not considered to be part of the holiday. Night-time accommodation is in a couchette – six berths, in three tiers, to a compartment, with blanket and pillow supplied – or in T1, T2 or T3 cabins. As the names imply, these offer one (first class ticket only), two or three berths. Breakfast at the destination is included in the price of the ticket.

BY ROAD

Coaches and Buses

France has an extensive, long-distance coach system and good local bus services. Not surprisingly, the majority of long-distance coach services head for Paris.

Cars

France has an excellent network of autoroutes backed up by a good system of 'ordinary' routes. The south of the country is served by the **Autoroute du Soleil**, the A7, that links it with Paris and the Channel ports. The A7 follows the Rhône Valley to Orange, where the A9 leaves it to reach Nîmes. To the south of Salon, the A8 heads off east to Cannes and Nice, while the A7 continues south to Marseille and Toulon. French autoroutes are toll roads but they do offer a much quicker and, for those not used to driving on the right, safer way to travel. Quicker they may be, but it is still over 700 miles (1,100km) from the Channel to the south so allow several days for the journey.

ACCOMMODATION

The Côte d'Azur has accommodation ranging from the most luxurious hotels imaginable to small camp sites, and everything in between. All the local Tourist Offices have brochures on hotels and camping sites in their area. The French Government Tourist Office in your home country will also be able to supply information on hotels.

The guide to hotels is now also available on the Internet at: http://www.crt-riviera.fr

Smaller hotels, usually in country areas and guaranteeing a menu made with mainly local produce belong to the **Logis de France** scheme. **Gîtes de France** offers furnished accommodation for self-catering. Both these organisations can be found at:

55 Promenade des Anglais
BP 1602
06011 Nice Cedex 1

There are different telephone numbers for the two organisations:

Logis
☎ (04) 93 80 80 40,
Fax (04) 93 62 39 44
The national reservation number for Logis is ☎ (01) 45 84 83 84

Gîtes
☎ (04) 93 44 39 39
For reservations ☎ (04) 92 15 21 30,
Fax (04) 93 86 01 06

Young people can contact:
Centre Régional Information Jeunesse Côte d'Azur
19 Rue Gioffredo
06000 Nice
☎ (04) 93 80 93 93,
Fax (04) 93 80 30 33

ARTS AND CRAFTS

The French Riviera has an enviable reputation in the history of art and a wealth of art museums. To help the visitor with costs – as all French museums charge an entry fee – the **Art'Pass** has been introduced. This gives visitors entry to over 60 listed art museums on a single pass which can be bought for 3 or 7 days. Whichever pass is purchased it offers a phenomenal reduction in costs, even for those who could not foresee be able to (or wanting to) visit several dozen museums.

The artistic heritage is still apparent, with dozens of art galleries selling work by local artists and visitors frequently be offered works by pavement artists. There is a also a flourishing craft industry with potteries, glass studios, jewelry makers, stained glass window makers, wood carvers and turners, not to mention those who hand-paint T-shirts and other, more obscure, but equally interesting, crafts. Look out for leaflets in the local Tourist Information Centres or just watch for studios as you drive around.

CURRENCY REGULATIONS

The French unit of currency is the French franc. There are no restrictions on the import of French or foreign currency but amounts must be declared if bank notes worth in excess of 5,000 French francs are likely to be exported.

CUSTOMS REGULATIONS

Normal EEC customs regulations apply for those travelling from Britain. Normal European regulations apply for those travelling from North America.

DISABLED VISITORS

Not all the sites listed in this guide are accessible to disabled visitors. A list of those that are, not only in Côte d'Azur but in the whole of France, can be found in the publication *Touristes quand même! Promenades en France pour les voyageurs handicapés*. This excellent guide can be obtained from:

Comité National Français de Liaison pour la Réadaptiondes Handicapés 38 Boulevard Raspail, 75007 Paris.

The guide will be of interest not only to those with a physical handicap, but to the visually handicapped and visitors with a hearing difficulty.

ELECTRICITY

220v ac, 50 Hertz (cycles/sec) in most places. Some small areas are still at 110v ac. Adaptors will be needed by those people who do not use continental two-pin plugs at home.

FINANCES

All major credit cards (MasterCard, Visa, American Express etc) are taken at most large restaurants, hotels, shops and garages. Eurocheques and traveller's cheques (checks) are also accepted.

Banks are normally open from 9am-12pm, 2-4.30pm, Monday to Friday only. They close early on the day before a Bank Holiday.

HEALTH CARE

British visitors have a right to claim health services in France by virtue of EEC regulations. Form E111 – available from the Department of Health and Social Security – should be obtained to avoid complications.

American and Canadian visitors will need to check the validity of their personal health insurances to guarantee they are adequately covered. For emergency assistance, dial 19 in all towns. In country areas it may be necessary to phone the local gendarmerie (police).

Pharmacies, clearly marked with a green cross, can usually deal with minor ailments or advise people where to go if any additional help is needed.

HOLIDAYS

France has the following national holidays:

New Year's Day
Easter Monday
May Day
Ascension Day

VE Day – 8 May
Whit Monday
Bastille Day – 14 July
Assumption Day – 15 August
All Saints' Day – 1 November
Armistice Day – 11 November
Christmas Day

MEASUREMENTS

France uses the metric system. Conversions are:

1 kilogram (1,000 grams) = 2.2 pounds
1 litre (liter) = $1^3/_4$ pints
4.5 litres (liters) = 1 gallon
1.6 km = 1 mile
1 hectare = $2^1/_2$ acres (approx)

POST AND TELEPHONE SERVICES

Stamps (*timbres*) are available from post offices, which are normally open from 8am-7pm Monday to Friday and 8am-12pm on Saturday. In some smaller towns and villages, the post office may be shut for lunch, both the timing and the duration of the break being a local custom.

Telephones in France take coins rather than tokens.
The dial codes from France are:

Great Britain	19 44
Canada	19 1
USA	19 1

Remember to leave out the first zero of your home country number – eg to dial the French Government Tourist Office in London (020 7491 7622) from France, dial 19 44 20 7491 7622. Many telephone booths now take phonecards; buy the télécarte from post offices and where advertised on telephone booths. Calls can be received at phone boxes where the blue bell is shown.

Within France, remember that a new code system has recently been introduced. This divides the country into five regions and gives them an additional two-digit number. Thus all numbers in France now have 10 digits. South-east France, including the Riviera, is 04. Thus to dial a number in Nice it is now necessary to dial (within France) 04 followed by the 8 digit code. When telephoning from the UK the first 0 must be dropped (ie. 00 33 4 xx xx xx xx). The international code for Monaco is 377: there is no French area code on Monacan numbers.

Above: Watching the world at play, Promenade des Anglais, Nice
Below: Lovers on the Larvotto beach, Monte Carlo

Jardin Japonais, Monte-Carlo

SPORT

GOLF

There are a dozen or more 18-hole golf courses on the Riviera as well as a further ten or so 9-hole courses. The French Government Tourist Office publishes a booklet 'Golf in France' which lists the international standard courses, while local Tourist Offices have information on courses in their area.

HORSE RIDING

For riding tuition or excursions contact:

Le Relais des Templiers
Quartier St Bernard
Levens, ☎ 93 79 71 95

La Ferme d'Anaïs
1 Avenue de la Borde
Mougins, ☎ 92 92 29 65

Centre Hippique de Mougins
909 Chemin de Font de Curault
Mougins, ☎ 93 45 75 b81

Cercle Hippique St Georges
2359 Route de Grasse
Villeneuve-Loubet, ☎ 93 20 99 64

MOUNTAIN SPORTS

The peaks of Alpes-Maritime and the Mercantour Park are ideal for walking, climbing and canyoning, and a host of clubs are available to help the visitor get the best from the area. Many of these are in the Roya Valley – contact the Tourist Office in Tende – but Tourist Offices in other towns, particularly Sospel and St Martin Vésubie will also be able to help.

The same Offices will be able to help with white water expeditions in the Loup and Roya valleys.

PARAGLIDING

The hills north of the sea are ideal for paragliding, offering a consistent updraft and, usually, excellent visibility. To give it a try, contact:

Ascendance
Auberge de Gourdon
Gourdon, ☎ 93 77 64 24

Cumulus
32 Avenue Prince de Galles
Nice, ☎ 93 38 25 92

Azur Vol Libre
372 Chemin du Bosquand
Bar-sur-Loup, ☎ 93 09 44 54

Roquebrune'Aile
14 Avenue Louis Laurens
Roquebrunne-Cap-Martin
☎ 93 35 00 68

ABC d'Air
1 Avenue Jéan Médecin
Sospel, ☎ 93 04 05 15

TENNIS/SQUASH

Most of the larger hotels and virtually all of the towns have tennis and squash courts. Ask at your local Tourist Information Office for details.

Fact File

TOURIST OFFICES

11 Place du Général de Gaulle
Antibes, ☎ 92 90 53 00

Nautisme et Tourisme
9 Rue Espirt Violand
Cannes, ☎ 92 18 88 88

Maison de la Mer
Route du Bord de Mer
Madelieu-La Napoule
☎ 93 49 88 77

Office du Tourisme
20 Avenue Paul Doumer
Roqubrunne-Cap-Martin
☎ 93 35 49 70

WATER SPORTS

With a clear, warm sea it is no surprise that water sports figure highly in the sports on offer. All the main beaches, particularly in Nice and Cannes, have private sections where visitors will be able to take a parachute ride behind a motor boat or borrow some limited water sports equipment. For the real enthusiast the *Pass Nautique Découverte* is a must, a pass which gives a 30 per cent discount on any new activity tried by the visitor at a (long) list of resorts. The pass is remarkably cheap and available from Tourist Offices .

The main stations for
water sports are:

Diving

Cap Plongée
Boulevard Wylie
Antibes, ☎ 93 67 26 22

Les Guides de la Mer
62 Avenue des Pins du Cap
Antibes, ☎ 93 61 45 45

Club Moana
Maison Maritime, Port du Cros
Cagnes-sur-Mer, ☎ 92 27 96 09

Centré Plongée Armand Ferrand
Port de la Rague
Mandelieu-La Napoule
☎ 93 49 74 33

Plongée International Centre
Port de Cannes Marina
Mandelieu-La Napoule
☎ 93 49 01 01

Club d'Exploration
Sous-Marine de Monaco
Jetée Sud, Quai des Sanbarbani
Monaco, ☎ 92 05 91 78

Europ'Sport
3 Promenade de la Mer
Menton, ☎ 93 35 95 83

Poséidon
Quai unel, Port de Nice
Nice, ☎ 93 55 09 95

Sub-Marine
14 Boulevard de Riquier
Nice, ☎ 93 89 84 63

Miramar deL'Esterel
Port Miramar
Thóule-sur-Mer, ☎ 93 75 48 51

Golfe Plongée Club
627 Chemin des Impiniers
Vallauris, ☎ 93 64 22 67

Loisirs SubAquatiques Détente
71 Boulevard des Frères Roustant
Vallauris, ☎ 93 63 15 45

Centre International de Plongée
Port Publique de Golfe-Juan,
Quai St Pierre
Vallauris, ☎ 93 63 65 19

École de Plongée
La Bastide, Avenue Léopold II
Villefranche-sur-Mer, ☎ 93 07 48 77

Sailing/ Windsurfing

Club Nautique d"Antibes
Port Vauban
Antibes, ☎ 93 65 80 00

Yacht-Club Beaulieu-sur-Mer
Quai Whitechurch
Beaulieu-sur-Mer
☎ 93 01 14 44

Société Nautique de Cagnes-sur-Mer
Port Abri du Cros-de-Cagnes
Cagnes-sur-Mer, ☎ 93 14 48 00

École Voile du Cros-de-Cagne
Port Abri du Cros-de-Cagnes
Cagnes-sur-Mer, ☎ 93 31 45 65

NEF (Nautisme et Formation)
37 Avenue des Chênes
Cagnes-sur-Mer, ☎ 93 07 20 62

Maison de la Mer
Route du Bord de Mer
Mandelieu-La Napoule
☎ 93 49 88 77

Yacht Club de Monaco
16 Quai Antoine 1er
Monaco, ☎ 93 30 63 63

Club Nautique de Nice
50 Boulevard Franck Pilatte
Nice, ☎ 93 89 39 78

Nereides École de Crisière
Port de St Laurent-du-Var
St Laurent-du-Var, ☎ 93 31 07 12

Wind Club
Atoll Plage,
Proemnade des Flots Bleus
St Laurent-du-Var, ☎ 92 27 14 51

Office Municipal des Sports
Quai Edouard Blondy
Théoule-sur-Mer, ☎ 92 97 56 32

Water Skiing

Water skiing is a little easier to find, but for solid instruction contact:

Sun Ski School
Parking du Vieux Port
Vallauris, ☎ 93 68 91 14

TIPPING

Tips (*pourboires*) are given as in your home country but in France they also apply to guides at both châteaux and museums.

TRAVEL BY CAR

Car Rental

Car rental is available from many companies, including all the well-known major European ones, and from all the big towns, the airports and all large railway stations.

Speed Limits

The speed limits currently applied to French roads are:

	In dry conditions	In the wet
Autoroutes	130kph (81mph)	110kph (68mph)
National (N) roads	110kph (68mph)	100kph (62mph)
Other roads	90kph (56mph)	80kph (50mph)
In towns	50kph (31mph)	50kph (31mph)

Note

There are new speed limits on autoroutes: a minimum of 50mph (80kph) for the outside lane during daylight, on level ground and with good visibility; and a maximum of 31mph (50kph) if the visibility is less than 55yd (50m).

No driving is permitted on a provisional licence and the minimum age to drive is 18. Stop signs mean exactly that – the vehicle must come to a complete halt.

It is compulsory for front seat passengers to wear seat belts and children below the age of 10 are not allowed to travel in the front seats. All vehicles must carry a red warning triangle and a spare headlamp bulb.

There are strict – and very strictly interpreted – laws on speeding and drink-driving. The former will usually result in an on-the-spot fine, while the latter will usually result in confiscation of the car.

In built-up areas, the motorist must usually give way to anybody coming out of a side-turning on the right. This is indicated by the sign, *priorité à droite*. However, this rule no longer applies at roundabouts which means vehicles already on the roundabout have right of way (*passage protégé*). All roads of any significance outside built-up areas have right of way.

Parking

Car parking is no easier in French towns than it is in most other large European cities. The by-laws vary from town to town and, occasionally, from day to day. To be safe it is best to use car parks. Check before leaving your parked car: it is common practice to take your ticket with you, to pay as you return and to use the stamped ticket or token to raise the exit barrier. If you drive to an exit and then discover this rule, it is likely that you will have a queue of cars behind you when you are trying to work out what has gone wrong or are trying to reverse. Since tokens are time-limited, the queue is unlikely to be sympathetic.

USEFUL ADDRESSES

Consulates-General

Great Britain
24 Avenue du Prado
Marseille, ☎ 91 53 43 32

USA
9 Rue Armeny
Marseille, ☎ 91 54 92 00

1 Rue du Maréchal-Joffre
Nice, ☎ 93 88 89 55

Canada
24 Avenue du Prado
Marseille, ☎ 91 37 19 37/37 19 40

French Government Tourist Offices

Great Britain
178 Piccadilly
London W1V 0AL
☎ 020 7493 6594

USA
444 Madison Avenue
New York
NY 10022, ☎ 212 838 7800

676 North Michigan Avenue
Suite 3360
Chicago, IL60611-2819
☎ 312 751 7800

(USA continued)

9454 Wilshire Boulevard
Suite 715
Beverley Hills, CA 90212-2967
☎ 310 271 2693

Canada
30 St Patrick's Street
Suite 700
Toronto ONT
M5T 3A3, ☎ 416 593 4723

1981 Avenue McGill College
Tour Esso Suite 490
Montreal PQ
Quebec
H3A 2 W9, ☎ 514 288 4264

Tourist Offices in France

Almost all towns and many villages have their own *Syndicats d'Initiative* and these will supply local information and maps.

The main offices are listed below.

Cannes
Palais des Festivals
☎ 93 39 24 53

Monaco
2A Boulevard des Moulins
☎ 92 16 61 16

Nice
Gare SNCF
Avenue Thiers
☎ 93 87 07 07

5 Promenade des Anglais
☎ 93 92 14 48 00

VISAS

No visa is required for holders of British, American and Canadian passports.

Only the main events are given here. It is worth checking with the local Tourist Office as new events are constantly being added to the schedules of the major, and many minor, resorts.

Antibes

Sunday after 29 June, **Festival of St Peter**, procession to Harbour

Cannes

February, **mimosa festival**

March, **photography and amateur cinema festival**

May, **international film festival**

July-August, *Nuits des Leirins*

August, **fireworks festival**

September, **international yachting festival; royal regattas**

September, **festival of vintage cars**

October-November, **international golf championships**

Digne

First Sunday in August, **lavender festival**

Entrevaux

Weekend nearest 24 January, **festival of St John the Baptist**
Two weeks in August, **sixteenth- and seventeenth-century music festival**

Fréjus

Third Sunday after Easter, *bravade* costume procession

Grasse

Last two weeks of July, **international amateur music, folk and drama festival**

Ile Ste Marguerite

1 June to 15 September, *son-et-lumière* at fort

Menton

Week before Shrove Tuesday, **lemon festival**

First two weeks of August, **international festival of chamber music** in floodlit Place de l'Eglise

Monaco

January, **Monte-Carlo motor rally**

27 January, **festival of Ste Dévote**

February, **international television festival**

April, **international tennis championships**

May, **Monaco Grand Prix**

July to August, **international fireworks festival**

August to September, **world amateur theatre festival**

November, **Monégasque National Festival**

December, **international circus festival**

Nice

Two weeks before Lent, Carnival, **fireworks display** (Shrove Tuesday), **Battle of Flowers** (day after Ash Wednesday)

April, **international dog show**
Each Sunday in May, *Fête des Maïs* in Cimiez Gardens

May, **spring music festival**

July, **grand jazz parade** in Cimiez Gardens

July, **international folklore festival**

August, **wine festival** in Cimiez Gardens

October, **autumn music festival**

Roquebrune-Cap-Martin

Good Friday evening, **procession of the Entombment of Christ**

Afternoon of 5 August, **procession of the Passion**

St Paul

Second fortnight in July, *Nuits de la Fondation Maeght*

St Tropez

16-18 May, *Bravade de St Torpes*

15 June, *Fête des Espagnols*, the Spanish *bravade*

Once a month in July and August, **classical concerts** in Citadel

Vence

Easter Sunday and Monday, **Battle of Flowers**, Provençal dancing

LANDMARK
VISITORS GUIDES

US & British VI*
ISBN: 1 901522 03 2
256pp,
UK £11.95 US $15.95

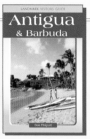

Antigua & Barbuda*
ISBN: 1 901522 02 4
96pp,
UK £5.95 US $12.95

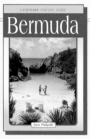

Bermuda*
ISBN: 1 901522 07 5
160pp,
UK £7.95 US $12.95

Dominican Republic*
ISBN: 1 90152208 3
160pp,
UK £7.95 US $12.95

Pack 2 months into 2 weeks with your Landmark Visitors Guides

New Zealand*
ISBN: 1 901522 36 9
320pp
UK £12.95 US $18.95

India: Goa
ISBN: 1 901522 23 7
160pp,
UK £7.95

India: Kerala
ISBN: 1 901522 16 4
256pp,
UK £10.99

Orlando*
ISBN: 1 901522 22 9
256pp,
UK £9.95 US $15.95

Florida: Gulf Coast*
ISBN: 1 901522 01 6
160pp
UK £7.95 US $12.95

Florida: The Keys*
ISBN: 1 901522 21 0
160pp,
UK £7.95 US $12.95

St Lucia*
ISBN: 1 901522 28 8
144pp,
UK £6.95 US $13.95

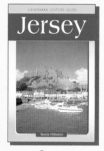

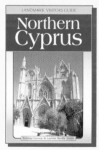

INDEX

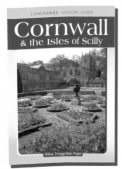
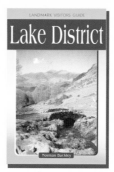
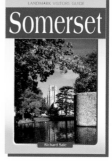

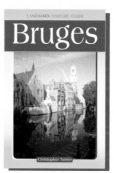
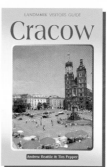

Published in the UK by
Landmark Publishing Ltd,
Waterloo House, 12 Compton, Ashbourne, Derbyshire DE6 1DA England
Tel: (01335) 347349 Fax: (01335) 347303 e-mail: landmark@clara.net

Published in the USA by
Hunter Publishing Inc,
130 Campus Drive, Edison NJ 08818
Tel: (732) 225 1900, (800) 255 0343 Fax: (732) 417 0482

1st Edition
ISBN 1 901 522 29 6
© Richard Sale 2000

British Library Cataloguing in Publication Data: a catalogue record for this book is available from the British Library.

Print: Gutenberg Press Ltd, Malta
Cartography: James Allsopp
Design: James Allsopp

Front cover: The beach at Larvotto, Monte Carlo
Back cover, top: Prince's Palace, Monaco
Back cover, bottom: La Croisette, Cannes
Page 1: Villefranche-sur-Mer from the Corniche Inférieure

Picture Credits
All photographs are supplied by Richard Sale

DISCLAIMER
While every care has been taken to ensure that the information in this book is as accurate as possible at the time of publication, the publishers and author accept no responsibility for any loss, injury or inconvenience sustained by anyone using this book.